ASHLEY JOHNSON

Serial Killer, Con artist & Jelena

A Jelena Cohert Series

First published by Forever Seven Press 2024

Copyright © 2024 by Ashley Johnson

All rights reserved. No part of this publication may be reproduced, stored or transmitted in any form or by any means, electronic, mechanical, photocopying, recording, scanning, or otherwise without written permission from the publisher. It is illegal to copy this book, post it to a website, or distribute it by any other means without permission.

This novel is entirely a work of fiction. The names, characters and incidents portrayed in it are the work of the author's imagination. Any resemblance to actual persons, living or dead, events or localities is entirely coincidental.

Second edition

ISBN: 979-8-9856989-0-9

Editing by Shelley Lopez

This book was professionally typeset on Reedsy. Find out more at reedsy.com

Contents

Prologue	1
She's Lying	3
Dan's on to something	6
Agent Cohert	8
Lunch	16
Hello, my name is Sandra Highworth	20
MDPD	25
Jane Stoneybrooke	34
Basement	47
I watched as she inhaled sharply, her eyes darted from one...	49
Angry Zumba	52
Break it down	62
Happy Hour	74
Sandra and Smith welcome to the family	84
Torture, poke and prod	93
Sorry, not sorry, move on	97
Daddy, I need your help	112
Wolf in sheep's clothing	118
Groundwork	133
Old and new crimes	146
You cannot die on accident	156
Is something wrong?	159
Where is Jelena?	170

Find my daughter!	179
The plan has changed	186
Follow the trail	200
She's alive, but will she live?	221
About the Author	227
Also by Ashley Johnson	229

Prologue

"¡Ayudame, it's dark!" I blink. I realize my eyes are open, I sense them opening and closing. "Why can't I see?!" Sobbing into the darkness. "I don't know where I am?" I claw to uncover something, anything that will give me a sign of where I am. I recover nothing but a hard, smooth surface. I stand up, and I get jerked back down. "Ah mi Dios" my neck "I have a choker on a chain." I claw and pull the chain, struggling to get loose. But I can't. I am chained up, like a slave or a creature. "Tied up like a dog." I slump down onto the floor, defeated.

Jelena panics. Breathing heavily, her palms are darting out and around trying to feel something that can save her. She stands and YANK back down to the ground. At last, she notices the chain, the anchor around her neck. Her elegant long neck, tethered to the floor, to my floor, to me. She doesn't see me standing at the bottom of the stairs studying her. Drinking in my particular brand of nutrients. I grin as I hear her whimpers. My grin widens as she scratches and pulls; willing the chain to move even an inch. I show all 32 as she slumps and weeps, allowing me to feed off her powerlessness and bask in the glory of her misery.

She's Lying

"Dan, have you seen my folder with the graded papers in it!?" Jelena hustles through the kitchen into the dining space, trying to locate her folder. She looks around, checking behind the potted plants and underneath the magazines and opening mail. "It's red honey!"

She added as she trips over the leg of the four seater table and stubs her toe. "Shit" she mumbles then pulls out the closest chair to sit and takes off her shoe to rub her feet.

The chair gets caught on the rug and Jelena has to jerk it to have the pull out enough for her to sit in it. The force from the moment almost knocks her over, and she hits her toe again as her foot raises up to catch her balance.

She sits down and rubs her throbbing toe when she hears her phone beep from another room.

Jelena jumps up, puts her shoe back on and is getting ready to call Dan's name again when he comes waltzing into the dining area holding a purple folder. She collides with him and he puts his arms to steady her so she doesn't fall over.

He chuckles "Whoa there, I got you" she notices the folder in his hands and stands with her mouth gaping open "close your mouth babe, you'll catch flies." She snaps her mouth shut and scowls. "So, you didn't hear me screaming?" She says as she reaches for the file.

He jerks it aside and puts it over his head with a playful twinkle in his eye. She reaches for the folder again. He holds it higher, making her go on her tiptoes to reach it. Dan holds it just out of her reach. "Give it to me Dan," she said with mock politeness in her voice while she is holding her hand out. "Go on ahead and get it," Dan replied.

Jelena scowled and tried to keep it in place but ended up smirking and looking more like a pouting 4-year-old asking for a treat from her dad. She jumps, struggling to catch him off guard. Which is still too high for her 5"3 frame to Dan's 6"0 frame, even with her 4-inch heels on. She draws a deep breath and adjusts her pink blazer. With the sweetest tone she could muster, "Dan, please hand me the folder so I can go to work?"

She was working hard on keeping an innocent face when her phone beeped again. Dan's cocky grin switched to annoyance as he looked in the sound's direction. She took advantage of his distractedness and grabbed her folder.

She ran for the door and took her keys and phone out of the bowl in the entry hallway. She yelled "love you" as she ran out the door, not bothering to close it. Jelena hit the beeper and unlocked her silver Porsche, hopped in and sped away.

She knew she pissed him off without looking in the rearview mirror. When she gave in and looked she saw him standing there with his beat face visible, even from down the street.

Jelena continued to drive two blocks down, took a left turn at the stop sign and stopped 4 houses down on the right, in front of 1808 Warrington Ave.

She pulled into the driveway and hit the remote to open the garage. As the door slid open, she drove up, got out of her Porsche, and opened the trunk to get her briefcase and her tote bag. She walked over and got into a reinforced black SUV.

She threw her bags along with her phone into the passenger seat. As she pulls out of the garage, hitting the remote to bring the door sliding back down. Picking up her phone and redials the last number that called her.

She put the phone to her ear, a female voice says "Hello, is this Senior Agent Cohert?" Jelena replied "Yes, who is speaking?"

"You have a meeting that starts in 5 minutes, this call is a reminder since you are not in the building yet," Jelena scoffs "Thanks" she says and hangs-up. She makes sure her Bluetooth is connected and hits play on her playlist.

Dan's on to something

"Something's not right," Dan mumbled as he poured the waffle batter. He goes over to the trash can underneath the garbage disposal and pulls out his black notebook. He opens to a fresh page and writes:

August 7th, 2019

Today my wife, Jelena, packed black cargo pants, a black shirt with letters on it. The shirt was inside out so I couldn't make out the words. She also had some black sneakers I didn't know existed until a few weeks ago. Out of 15 years of marriage, the first time I've seen those sneakers were last month. When I went into the bathroom, she was stuffing the clothes in the duffel bag. By the time I got out of the shower, the bag had disappeared.

This is day 3 of Jelena asking for a red folder and me bringing her a different color folder and her taking it like it was her mistake. The red folder has grades in it with Mabel Simmons with a B+, Leroy Brown with a C- and Cora Simmons with an A. What type of fool does she take me for!

Dan slams the notebook back in its spot and puts the trash can back on top of it. He does this so hastily he doesn't realize that the trashcan was uneven. Dan slams the cabinet door and then jumps when the beeper for the waffle iron went off "Dammit" he scolded himself.

He walks over, opens the machine and pulls the waffle out directly from the iron. Then he jumps back dropping the waffle "DAMMIT" he screams.

He goes over to the sink sucking his finger and then runs icy water on it. Then unplugs the waffle iron and pick up his mess off the floor, throwing it in the trash. He goes searching for his phone and ends up in the bedroom. He grabs his phone off of his side table and goes through his messages and emails. There are a lot of promotional emails.

As he scrolls nothing catches his eye, so he closes the email and opens up his text messages. There's a text from his boss telling him to get into the office immediately.

Dan swears and checks the time on the text. He rushes to get his things together, noticing he got the message over 40 minutes ago. He rushes downstairs and out the door.

Agent Cohert

Jelena pulls into the building parking lot on 145th Avenue and hustles into the office building, making a beeline for the conference room. She hates all the stares she gets.

These men are thinking they may undress me with their eyes. Yes, I'm sort of in shape, I'm not out of shape but don't exercise either.

I dyed her hair honey blonde to get rid of the chocolate I've had all my life. My eyes are green, like an olive green. It was rough being picked on all my life for not being Latina enough because I had white people's eyes.

The rumors about my father and mother cheating also got to me. It didn't help that both of my siblings, a brother and a sister both had brown or hazel eyes.

My face is chubby and I am a size 12, with a good hourglass shape though.

I looked good; I guess. "They don't need to be staring at me like that though" she mumbles in Spanish and she rolls her eyes.

She gets to the correct room and opens the door; conversations stop, and all eyes turn to her. "Well, well, well Mrs. Cohert nice of you to join us" Jelena scowls at the other senior agent.

She shuts the door behind her, slamming it harder than necessary and goes to the empty chair across the room. "Nothing to say for yourself Mrs. Cohert?" Senior Agent Peter Romanary says looking smug in the front of the room.

"You may continue, Mr. Romanary." The Senior Agent drops his smirk and scowls, "That's Senior Agent Romanary to you." Jelena uncrosses and re-cross her legs while holding his stare "likewise."

SA Romanary clears his throat and adjusts his suit jacket. "Well, thank you Senior Agent Cohert for joining us." Spitting out her name as if he had poison on his tongue. "As I was saying before you joined our meeting" he said with an emphasis on the word joined "we are starting a task force to work full time on Sandra Highworth."

Cohert glanced around the room and noticed the 7 people in total. First, there was Romanary and herself, the Senior Agents.

There were also four other agents in the room, three of which were male. She made an audible scoff and rolled her eyes. Romanary glared at her and she stared daggers into him and apologized "excuse me" and her most mocking tone.

Special Agents Chad Bell and Jared Belle are to her right, half-brothers. Long story short, papa was a rollin' stone and added an extra E at the end of Belle and family number two to hide them from Bell and family number one.

Special Agent Swift Jonathan is young and green but with Special Forces experience.

Then there's her best friend, Angela Rodríguez. They bonded because they were the only females in the unit. because they were Latina. *She's the only one who knows about me and my past,* Cohert thinks. She calls me a sellout because I married a white man. That almost made her chuckle, but she swallowed it. *Wouldn't want to interrupt again,* she thought, rolling her eyes.

"Anything to add Cohert" the irritating voice disrupts her thoughts. She turned her attention back to the room.

"Since I wasn't listening, I will bullet point a few things. I am leading this task force. Regardless of what Romanary has said or left unclear. It will not be our entire team. I will take three of you and we will join three members of Miami Dade Police Department. Headquarters will be in a location I debrief the three of you who I choose to be on the task force." Cohert looks to her right, the 7th member of the team, her Boss. "Anything to add Boss?"

At the mention of his name he stands up and buttons the button on his suit jacket. "Dismissed." Cohert makes her way over to Rodriguez and hugs her friend. She eyes her Boss leaving the room and Romanary close behind him, not looking happy at all. She laughs and turns towards Rodriguez. "¡Chica, usted le dijo!" <Girl, you told him>

"Uh sir, can I have a word, please?" Romanary asks. They reach the corner office, and Boss sighs and waves Romanary in after him. He sits and swivels his chair to face his agent.

"Yes, Cohert is lead, because I said so. Yes she has the choice of adding you to the team or not, whatever she decides will be non negotiable." Boss stares at him unwavering awaiting a response.

Romanary knows better and says "yes sir" tight lipped and left the office. He squints his eyes and looks and the direction of Cohert's office door. He mumbles "you bitch" and then he makes a beeline to Cohert's office.

Cohert and Rodriguez are sitting on the couch in Cohert's office. Romanary comes barging in. The ladies stop talking, stare at each other and then at the door.

"Excuse me, the door was closed which means you knock and await a response before entering," Cohert says with attitude.

She then turns back to Rodriguez and says "el descaro" Rodriguez agrees "Right girl! The nerve!"

Romanary stands in the doorway with a beat red face. He spits "English immigrants" and then turns and leaves the room. Once he has left the room Cohert gets up and locks her door.

Romanary starts banging on the door and twisting the knob, "Cohert open the damn door!" "Lo siento señor, no hablo inglés," <Sorry sir, I don't speak English> Cohert turns and walks back over to her couch, the two women laughing. "Are you not going to let him in?" Rodriguez asks as she glances at the door.

"He is still banging," she said mischievously. "Niña mi Dios," <My God girl> she says chuckling. "He'll be okay, he is coming to tell me I better put him on the task force, and I'm not. It will be you, J. Belle, Jonathan."

#

Cohert brings her file folders and briefcase into the conference room and sets them on the table. She stares around the table at Rodriguez, Belle, and Jonathan.

"Agents, you are my task force" she says with pride in her voice as she passes identical tablets and folders around the table. "These tablets are for the Highworth case, no other information is to be stored on these. Sandra Highworth is a con woman, a con artist or whatever you want to call it; I'd venture to say the best con of anything since Dewitt of 77'. She has been on the international radar for the past 2 decades. The most recent being the jewelry heist at The Grand Ball last year."

The agents flip through the file folders and swipe through

the provided tablets, taking in the information as agent Cohert continued the rundown.

"She walked away with over 150 million dollars and no one knew someone had stolen anything until the next day when the Museum was opened. I need everyone to become best friends with her file. We leave for MDPD in 45 minutes." When no one had questions, she began packing her things.

Everyone gathered their materials and headed to their cubicles. Romanary came into the room and closed the door behind him. Standing in front of the door, blocking it, arms folded across his chest with an intense scowl on his face.

"Si señor como puedo ayudarte -" <Yes sir, How can I help you> "Cut the Spanish shit, Cohert," he interrupts. "Why the hell didn't you include me on that meeting, on this task force I am Senior Agent around here whether you like it or not!"

"Lo siento señor no hablo inglés, solo soy un inmigrante." <Sorry sir, I don't speak English. I'm only an immigrant> she says looking at him innocently.

"Inmigrante" he says butchering the Spanish word "Cut the crap immigrant" he spits out "and catch me up to speed." He stares at her, daring her to go against him.

Romanary sits in the chair closest to her, after he thinks he's won the staring contest. Like he deserves an "atta boy" for his aggressive prejudice and racist comments. His arms still crossed, and he stared up at her with a smirk on his lips.

Cohert leans close to his face. "You are not my superior. I do not say how high when you say jump." She stands and walks over to the door and opens it "you are not on my task force, my task force," She enunciates.

That last bit got him, face turning beat red he jumped up from his chair and stomped out of the conference room like a

3-year-old who got his toy taken.

Cohert walk back to her office, dumped all her stuff on her chair and started organizing things and putting them into her briefcase preparing to leave. Boss walked in and sat on the edge of her desk.

"Yes, sir," she said, not faltering from her current task. "I had to come see why one of my Senior Agents is throwing items around in his office and screeching. It's a tantrum, I needed to see why one of my Senior Agents was throwing a tantrum."

She stopped moving for a second and chuckled, then continued with her task. Walking across the room she says, "No se señor." <I don't know sir>

The Boss smirked with the sudden understanding. "The Spanish, that's what got him." Boss says letting a sound escape his lips that sounded like a chuckle. "Well Cohert," he continued "good luck on this, you'll need it. No mistakes, no cutting corners, all the T's crossed and I's dotted," he said.

"Got it sir" she said as she threw her briefcase over her shoulder. The Boss got the cue and got up and walked to her door. She followed her Boss out and closed her office door, waiting until she heard a click before walking away.

#

Cohert pulls up to 117th avenue, MDPD headquarters, and walks towards her team who she sees waiting by the side of the building.

"We ready?" She says as she reaches them. She looks to each member of her team.

"Sí muchacha,"

"yes ma'am," Jonathan, Belle and Rodriguez say in unison.

They walk into the building and are greeted by a tall man. He has salt and pepper hair. *Kind of George Clooney - ish*, Cohert thinks as she extended her hand.

"Hello, I'm Senior Agent Cohert, this is my team agent's Jonathan, Belle and Rodriguez." She says as she looks at the members as she's naming them. The members of her team also nod at him upon hearing their name.

"SA Cohert hello I'm Captain Cross, follow me this way and I'll bring you to the detectives you'll be working with."

They Walk into the building and Belle replies comments "This looks almost as good as our place." Cohert looks back at him with a mixture of a scowl and a smirk and then turns back around to pay attention to where she is going.

They enter a sizable room with three men sitting around a small table. There are two more similar small tables in the room in one table that's at least double the size of the smaller ones.

"Gentleman" Captain Cross waves the agents in. "This is SA Cohert and her team, Rodriguez, Belle and Jonathan." He introduces the agents as they walk in. Cohert gets right down to business.

She takes three tablets and file folders out of her briefcase and hands them one by one to the detective. "Pleasantries later detectives," She says in a no-nonsense tone. "This is everything we have on Sandra Highworth. The tablets are clean and are to only be used for this case. Do not store any other information on these tablets."

"There is a GPS map on your tablet with an address already saved on it. We will break for lunch and meet at HQ in 2 hours. Bring what you need, nothing more." She stops and looks to see if anyone has questions. Turning to Captain Cross "thank you Captain, I'll be in touch." She shakes his hand and turns on her heels. Her team stays back and chats with the detectives.

On her way out, she took the time to admire the building. *Belle was right, she* thought. The building is filled with flat screens and monitors. There were people scattered back and forth getting work done, having conversations, and even yelling at each other. The walls were glass so there was complete transparency except for the office doors. As she walked outside, she turned and looked at the building. She noticed that it looks like any other office building on the street. *I bet they had that in mind when they made the design*; she thought.

Lunch

Jelena parks 4 blocks away from Vero Italian and walks the distance to get to the door. *I didn't have enough time to go home and switch the cars*; She thinks, which means she definitely wouldn't afterwards.

"God was Italian the best choice, this walk back will be a workout," She mumbled. Dan jogs over to her. "I was getting worried Jelena you're late." He says as he leans in and kisses her on the cheek.

"Sorry Hun, I had to take a Lyft because I drove with Rodriguez to - I just didn't have my car." Jelena says to prevent herself from having to make up yet another lie.

Together they walk up to the host "Hello, reservation for Cohert" Dan says. The host looks through the book and says "right this way". They get led through the restaurant to a booth near the back. They take their seats and Dan looks at her, almost suspiciously.

"What" she says looking at him. "It's just weird that you didn't have your car" he says trying to sound nonchalant. Jelena rolls her eyes and sighs heavily.

"Mi Dios Dan, what's up with that?"

Dan rolls his eyes "enough with the Spanish, I hate that. What's up with what?"

"You have been questioning everything lately." She says with the menu in her hand. She is absently flipping pages as she continues. "I get the third degree every time I see you."

"Third Degree," Dan says rather loudly. He notices and adjusts his voice level before speaking again. "Exaggerating, are we? What's wrong with me being concerned that my wife is taking a Lyft and not driving the $60,000 Porsche I bought her. I'll take you back to work." He says matter-of-factly and picks up the menu. Trying to end the conversation.

"Please Dan, I can afford my lifestyle with or without you," Jelena says pointedly.

Dan signs and begins, "No you cannot. Plus, you know that's not what I meant -"

Jelena cuts him off, "I don't care what you meant." She set down the menu and looked at him. "I can afford a Porsche and I can manage a 15-minute Lyft ride."

"I am not your student Jelena, don't speak to me as if I am,"

Jelena sighs an exaggerated sigh, "Ah mi Dios Dan are we going to do this or are we going to eat lunch?"

Dan scoffs "English, speak English! That's another thing, why do they have you doing your classes at the FBI building, why not a university like a normal teacher? That makes no sense."

Jelena, slightly relieved, picked up the menu again. Attempting for a second time to look through it. "I work for the FBI Dan, not the University. A class taught by an FBI agent as to be in the FBI building"

He chuckles, "Oh, so you're special because you're an FBI agent, too bad you don't get to do any field work," Jelena forces a chuckle.

"Hello ma'am, sir, my name is Anna and I will be your server"

She says looking back and forth at the two of them. The 20 something year old, caramel skin waitress says "Can I start you off with something to drink?"

"Uh, what wine do you suggest?" Dan asks."The Pinot Grigio would go great if you're having Alfredo. The Zinfandel would be great with our other menu options."

"We will have the Pinot Grigio please and allow us a few moments to review the menu." The waitress scribbled on her pad, smiled and headed away into the crowd. Dan catches Jelena looking at him and shrugs "what?"

"Is this 1910 and I cannot order my drink?" He rolls his eyes and goes back to looking at the menu. Jelena stares at him, offended he ordered for her. He rarely does that, she thought he knows better.

"Please Jelena really? Come on now don't be that way." He looks up at her again when he notices she has not moved to get her menu, or moved at all. He puts the menu down and looks at her. "Why are you being testy about this?" He asks folding his hands together on the table really giving her his attention.

"I was just kidding Dan Geesh, don't have a heart attack," she says, not wanting to cause a scene.

He stares at his wife two seconds longer and then picks his menu back up. "What are you feeling babe?" Jelena asks him, letting out the breath she was holding. The waitress comes back with the wine and the couple order their food. The next hour and a half go smooth. The conversations and banter returned to a normal they are both comfortable with.

Dan walks Jelena outside adamant on waiting for my Lyft. So, she pulls out her phone and orders a Lyft to take her the four blocks to her car. Let me get to work, she thought as she climbed into a blue Prius.

#

Rodriguez sat in the police station with the three detectives. Michaels, Clearweather and Firestone were all vets. Michaels was about 5'10 with sandy brown hair and hard features. Clearweather was a fine shade of mocha, bald and had to be over 6'0. The man was tall. Then there was Firestone, Firestone was brown skinned with a brush cut. He was somewhere north of the other detectives, taller than all of them, and Rodriguez thought he was fine!

Hello, my name is Sandra Highworth

Sandra walked out of the Mandarin Oriental as the doorman told her to have a wonderful day.

"Will do, thanks love" she says in a French accent and walks to the awaiting car brought by the valet. With her chocolate hair blowing in the breeze, she jumps into the convertible and speeds down the street.

She heads to Surf & Turf Catering to get something to eat. She pulls onto Brickell Avenue and parks on the side in front of the First Presbyterian Church Parking lot. She gets out of the car and checks her surroundings. She crosses the street to the restaurant, noticing the cars, people and buildings around her. She walks in and looks around, finding her date she walks up to Jake Blaten.

The epitome of tall, dark and handsome, she stands and just admires him for a few seconds. It's been a long time, she thinks. She catches his eye half way through his Mike Special. His smile is sloppy and the tartar sauce dripping from his chin weirdly made him even more irresistible. As she passes a waitress, she asks in her Boston accent for a milkshake and slides into the booth.

"Well, to what do I owe this surprise, it's been a long time" Jake says with a mouth full of food. The waitress comes with her milkshake and asks her if she wants to order any food. Never one to turn down food, Sandra orders the lobster shrimp and fish. The waitress takes her order and then hustles away.

"I need a favor" Sandra says in her original accents, with a slight southern drawl, once the waitress is out of earshot. She slurps the milkshake. His eyebrows go up and he chuckles as he takes another bite, "are we in a position to be asking for favors?"

"I need a husband and a month. In return you'll get a couple million, sounds like a plan?" She says nonchalantly. He puts his fork down and studies her closely.

"Where have you been?" He says not breaking eye contact with her.

She sighs and rolls her eyes "a little here and a little there ya know. The things you must do when you're internationally wanted." she chuckles, but Jake doesn't laugh.

"So, what are you doing here?" Jake emphasizes the word here.

"A guy owed me a favor." She shrugs indifferently, and this makes Jake chuckle.

"And when you called in this favor your friend erased your face from all databases, huh?" He resumed eating his food.

"When anyone searches my name, nothing will show up, I have no criminal record. Now all I gotta do is stay out of trouble and I can live how I want."

Jake snorted, "Don't you already live how you want?"

Sandra winked at him and took another slurp of her milkshake.

"And needing me for a husband and a month is staying out of trouble?" He asks while he laughs humorously.

The waitress brought her food, and she digs in. She has never been the girl who nibbles on a piece of lettuce. She glances up occasionally and Jake is staring intently at her; she continues to eat.

"I can't figure out" she says in between chewing "whether you are trying to think over my proposal or judging the way I eat." His mouth hangs open for a few beats, like he can't quite figure out what to say. This makes her snort. She then coughs up the food she just inhaled.

Finally, he says "I'm staring because I don't know where all that food you shovel in goes to" he says looking her up and down. She snorts and says "I have a high metabolism" He laughs out loud and holds his heart for dramatic effect "Oh, that's your secret."

She laughs but doesn't let that interrupt her momentum with eating. "Okay, let me hear the plan" He says before taking the last bit of this sandwich and chewing it loudly with his mouth open.

"Okay," she says, pushing the food in her mouth to one side to chew. "In 4 weeks there is an auction of Danielle Prices' belongings in her estate."

He chokes on his water "you mean oil Danielle Price, she died?"

"No, she is about to die though. She wants to sell all her things and donate the money to charity so her selfish kids have nothing to fight over. She plans on auctioning her things and selling her house within the next month. She has already handed over her shares of the company to some longtime family friend who has been working in the company since he was 16, working his way up and shit like that." She slurps the last bit of the milkshake, then slurps her last piece of lobster. She pushed the dishes to the end of the table and looked at Jake.

"So, we need to get into that auction and drive the prices up on anything and everything. Once the auction is finished there is a 30-minute window we have to hack into their system and steal the money."

Jake shakes his head "wait hold on, no one gives the money immediately. It will take days for all the money to transfer."

She smirks and waves her finger back and forth "Oh the contrary, at this auction the winner of the piece must transfer the cost of the piece immediately after each article closes. So, we will have a 30-minute window to hack into the system, and take the money before the company's system is finished its transfer process. We need to interrupt that process and reroute the money to go into one of my offshore accounts. The auction house will check the amount, take their fee and there will be no more money left in the open auction account. We need to be out of there as soon as the money is transferred to my account." As they stand Jake puts two twenty-dollar bills on the table.

They walk out of the restaurant Jake is shaking his head and rubbing his chin. "I don't know Sandra there are a lot of steps to this and what if someone recognizes you?" He says as he holds the door open for her to exit.

She scoffs "I am no one to recognize, remember? Upstanding citizen Sandra Highworth." She chuckles, and then abruptly stops and looks at him. "We will have aliases though." She said as she threw Jake a set of keys. Sandra's Lyft pulls up and Jake looks at her with a crease in his brow "a Lyft, really?" He says pointing one hand in the car's direction.

"Hey a girl's got to get around right, I'll be in touch darling." She says returning to the French accent. He smiles, and she returns his smile and throws him the keys to her convertible.

Jake holds his stomach and erupts in laughter. He looks

around and pushes the key fob. The convertible makes noise, and he looks across the street at the car. "How long do I have in this?" He asks, still smiling.

"Uh, probably about another hour if so" she says with a wink "I came from the hotel straight here" she smiles as she hops into the car and rides off. She pulls out her phone and puts a check by 'get Jake'

MDPD

"Hello everyone, I am Senior Agent Cohert and I will lead this team," she said as she shifted from one foot to the next. "I've come to the understanding that everyone has gotten acquainted during lunch" she pauses "so we'll keep introductions short and get to work." Cohert looks to her left where detective Johnathan Michaels sits, he takes the hint and says

"Ma'am," he nods his head, "I'm Johnathan Michaels. I have been with one force of another for about 10 years." hearing his southern drawl coming through thickly. Once Michaels finishes; he and everyone at the table looks to Clearweather.

"I'm DC," the next man in line says "David Clearweather, I've just became a detective last year with 4 years on the MDPD before then."

"And I'm Cassidy Firestone. I am from London, as you can probably hear. 7 years on somebody's force 3 years as a detective." Firestone looked around the table, and his eyes landed on Rodriguez. She didn't turn her gaze. Firestone gave her a coy smile before turning his attention back to Cohert.

Cohert raised an eyebrow at her friend, and then looked around the room. "Very well, let's get to business. As you all can see we are in a house."

Cohert says while gesturing around for effect.

Belle scoffs and mumbles "More like a mansion" "si, una mansion" Rodriguez adds, looking around dramatically.

Cohert exhales forcefully "Yes, it's a sizeable house" she says in a light tone. She smiles at Rodriguez and then her tone gets serious.

"We are in Homestead, we needed something off the FBI and MDPD grounds to conduct our business to ensure complete privacy. It doesn't hurt to have a full kitchen and 5 bedrooms upstairs."

Rodriguez and Firestone lock eyes and break the moment quickly.

Cohert continues, "Sandra Highworth is an international con woman, and a damn good one. She has stolen billions of dollars across the United States and Europe over the last 2 decades." Cohert kicks off her heels and sits in the chair she was standing in front of. "Three weeks ago her name dropped from all of our databases. Everything from county to federal. We have picked her up on facial recognition at Miami International Airport so we know she is here."

Rodriguez spoke up "wait, when was she hacked off of the databases and if she was not on the wanted list how did facial recognition know to look for her face?"

Cohert crossed her legs, "The bureau is unsure of who the hacker is. The system didn't notify us, IT was just checking airports and train stations for the 10 most wanted."

"To your other question Rodriguez," Cohert began "IT pulled up the most wanted poster to take her picture from there for the program, to not have to go into her file. That's when he noticed she was not on the list anymore. He then looked at her file only to find that she no longer had none. She googled a picture of her to upload to the program and ran it immediately. Jimmy went to go tell is supervisor. When they came back to his computer, the program had a hit. Highworth has been in this country for the past week." Belle spoke up, "How the hell did someone hack her off our database? No pictures, no files, no nothing?"

Cohert shook her head, "I had interns go into the archives and scan anything paper we have on her. They are scanning and sending to me the ones I have not had delivered. Once I have them, I will share them," she reassured everyone. Firestone sits forward "We know she is here, let's just grab her."

"I wish. We need her to commit another crime. If we grab her now, with our evidence and case files deleted or buried, we will never win."

"We have on good authority that she will be at the auction of Danielle Price in a few weeks. We need to coordinate and be at that auction. We will arrest her after she steals the money. It has to be after, and we need proof of the theft. We need to know her entire plan, inside and out, she cannot be any steps in front of us. We also need to have complete cases on her previous money schemes, all put together by the time of her arrest. We also need to beef up the cases we already have. Make them court ready."

Cohert stood up, "Rodriguez and Firestone will work the auction angle. Clearweather and Jonathan will work the past scheme angle. Michaels and Belle will work all angles, dotting the T's and crossing I's making an airtight case. I will have my hands everywhere. Use me and critique me, bounce ideas off me. We are a team, let's act like it."

Everyone splits up and gets to work. The auction team, Rodriguez and Firestone, goes into the living room with boxes and folders. They sit on the couch and Rodriguez pulls out a legal pad.

"Okay, Angela," Firestone says "when is the auction?" Rodriguez stares at him for a moment, "let's keep it professional detective Firestone."

Rodriguez writes as she speaks, "The auction is four weeks away on a Saturday which would bring us to September 8th. Price is auctioning off her things so she can donate the money before she dies. She has cancer and not long left to live."

Firestone pulls a picture of Danielle Price out of one box and puts it on the whiteboard he pulled from the supplies in the kitchen. Underneath the picture he writes Danielle Price, 65, stage 4 cancer.

"Okay so why is she auctioning her things before she is dead?" Rodriguez searches through one box when she comes up empty she pulls out her phone "We will need to print out copies of these. But she recently has done an interview and said her kids are selfish and she does not want them to have a penny of her money."

She hands her phone to Firestone "so, she is selling her things and donating the proceeds to a few local charities around Miami." While she was talking, she had taken her computer out and printed off a copy of the article.

"Hold on a minute" she walks out of the room and returns with a piece of paper. She heads over to the board and tapes it under Price's picture.

"So how does one get an invitation to this auction?" Rodriguez asks.

"That's what we need to figure out first," Firestone says "let's get to work."

#

"Okay so how many known cons do we have Highworth for?" Clearweather asks to Belle, Jonathan and Michaels.

They brought a whiteboard out of a den area with supplies in it. He grabbed the whiteboard, some markers and tape. He walks over to the whiteboard and writes.

"The earliest one we know is the mall heist in 2000 where she went into a mall and stole from multiple department stores before authorities were alerted and she got away," Belle said. He set boxes on the table and took the notebook off the top of the first one.

Clearweather countered, "How do we know it was her?"

"Because her con was going into a store and picking up packaged things off the shelves" Belle read the notebook and looked on the side of the box. There was a number there. He reached for another box and saw the number five on the side and opened it. Belle pulled out a manila folder and looked through it. He shuffled through the paperwork and pulled out a copied page of handwritten notes.

He read "She would pre-pick stores with no return policy or a no receipt no return policy. She would walk up to the counter and ask for a return and subsequently get told no. She would say she understood and thank you anyway, ask for a bag and walk out of the store. The only reason she got caught is because when she went into her last store one employee saw her picking up the items. After the employee saw her walk out with a bag of the items, she asked the cashier how big of a commission she had gotten. The cashier explained it was a failed return and the other employee assured her she saw Highworth pick up the items. Then they sounded the alarm," Belle finished.

Clearweather scowled at Belle and then turned to the board

and wrote summer 2000 mall scheme.

"Okay, Michael's whatchu' got?" Clearweather said.

Michaels put down his tablet and looked up. "Okay, the next one appears to be in winter of 2005. For this one, she needed a hacker of some sort. We don't have all the information because the interns haven't sent over everything yet. So far I've got," he picked up his tablet and read from the screen.

"She walked into an investment firm and convinced them to keep her to hack into their systems to see where they needed to bump up security. Once she was hired, she stole all the money, transferred it into her account and then left. She got caught because they did a background check on her and a computer search revealed she never went to the University of Miami. Somehow, she was notified of the check and transferred as much as she could. She slipped out of her office as she heard security coming down the hall. Once she came off the elevator her hair was disheveled, and she looked disfigured. The guards at the front door let her pass without question."

Clearweather wrote 2005 investment con on the board. Jonathan made a sound of frustration "over the next 10 years it seems she did the rich husband thing until 2016 when paintings were replaced with fakes in California. However, we have plenty of proof of the 5 marriages but none on the painting, it was just assumed she did it." Clearwater added that to the side.

"If we cannot prove she did it I don't want us putting time and energy into it. That sounds good guys?"

"Uh, I'll keep it on my radar. I don't think we should completely take it off the board. The more evidence we have the better," Belle said.

Clearweather faced Belle "we have no proof though. Why spend time and energy that can be allocated elsewhere?"

Belle stopped and faced Clearweather. Giving him his full attention.

"Because it makes little sense that way," Clearweather said, raising his voice slightly.

Belle's voice remained calm and neutral, "As we go through all the other information and hit all of our sources we will see comes of it. Our case is better with all the schemes and cons. We have nothing solid on anything she has done from 2015 to that jewelry thing last year. So, you and Jonathan can work on the cases we know about and I will start on the ones we don't know for sure."

Michaels stood up, "yup sounds good to me. We have nothing to cross and dot until the rest of ya'll start handing us things."

They gathered their things and left. Clearweather stood there, upset.

"Let's get to work man" said Jonathan "the only cook here is Cohert, remember that." Jonathan stared at him with a raised eyebrow. Jonathan sat and got to work going through boxes.

Clearweather stood there an extra beat taking deep breaths trying to calm himself. I'm not trying to be the cook, he thought to himself, It just makes sense. I know I'm the rookie, but I will not be tossed around.

#

Cohert went up to one bedroom and got to work. She spent the day trying to follow the money. Where did all the money go, who did she sell the items to? When she looked up to check her phone, it was 4:30 pm.

"Damn it, 4:30," she hopped up and yelled through the house "Guys come let's do an info check before we head out for the day."

The team gathered in the kitchen with their tablets.

Rodriguez began, "we spent our day talking to Jones & Johnson and digging into Danielle Price's life and just digging. Trying to see what information we have and don't have and what info the interns have not sent us yet. Our to-do list is: run down Jones & Johnson's policy and procedures, figure out Highworth's plan by seeing what we would do to get the heist done and where is Highworth. We have those three things to start off with. We will be back in the afternoon tomorrow after we make a stop at the bureau building."

Belle spoke for him and Michaels, "We have been digging, and into the 2005 heist that we don't have a lot of information on. Our to-do list is: continue the search for evidence on the 2005 heist and dot the t's and cross the I's on the other cases when presented to us. We will meet at the bureau building in the am and see if the techs have any video in evidence that missed the hack."

Jonathan adjusted in his chair, "and that leaves us," he said. Looking down at his tablet he began "we spent our day going through the boxes and separating evidence into crimes. Out to-do list is: continue doing that, because we aren't done, print out everything being forwarded from the interns and separate them and organize a case file for each crime."

Cohert reached under the kitchen table for her shoes "My day comprised of a phone conversation with offshore banks and my to-do list is getting warrants for Hightworth's offshore accounts."

Cohert stood "Guys I got to head home, I have wife shit to do I'll see everyone tomorrow Adios Amigos!" and with that she was out the door.

Upon hearing that, everyone gathered their belongings and

headed to the door.

Firestone ran to catch up with Rodriguez. "Hey Angela," Firestone said grinning ear to ear, "Want to hit someone's happy hour?"

"Lo siento señor, I have plans already." She said with a twinkle in her eye.

"On a Tuesday?" he asks her eyes wide with surprise.

She winks at him and heads to her car "Lo siento" she said again.

"Damn that Spanish" Firestone mumbles to himself watching her walk towards her car.

Jane Stoneybrooke

The next morning Sandra sat in yet another hotel room. I am sick of hotels; it's been 3 days she thought. She was on the internet trying to search for recent articles of businesses being hacked, losing a lot of money. She searched for student loan debt or mortgage loans being erased and she found nothing; she groaned in frustration.

She spent three days looking, trying to find Slickey and could not find her anywhere. She never even thought of the possibility that Slickey had gone clean.

"Damn it" she said as she tossed her laptop on the couch next to the bed. Her phone chirped with a text message; she picked it up.

Jake: Hello wife
Sandra: Jake :)
Jake: How exactly are we supposed to get invited to this auction?
We need an actual invitation, we cannot just waltz in as the Joneses.
Sandra: First off honey we are not the Joneses, we are the Stoneybrooke's. Second, we need to go house shopping, this hotel

Is killing me. Meet me at 0818 Chestnut place in Sunny Isles Beach

In 25 minutes.

Jake: The Stoneybrooke's!! Like Miriam Stoneybrooke. Everyone knows her. How the hell

Are we going to pull this off?!

Sandra: See ya soon! Xoxo.

Sandra packed her belongings into her Michael Kors bag. She looked around the room one last time, checking to see if she'd left anything. She left the room and went to the front desk.

"Hello" she squints and stares at the young man's name tag "Steven, I'm Jane Stoneybrooke and I am checking out of suite 2558." She says in her French accent. The man clicks away at his computer.

"Okay Mrs. Stoneybrooke, can I have an ID and your payment method please?" Sandra waves her hand as if she's annoyed "no son look again, my information should already be linked to the account."

"Ma'am I have a Mrs. Miriam Stoneybrooke here but there is no payment method linked to the account."

Sandra scoffs "you silly boy my name is JANE J-A-N-E Stoneybrooke, I said that. The man apologizes and searches the computer again."

"My apologies again ma'am I see your account here. Now if I can just have an ID to close the stay out?" Sandra weeps dramatically and begins searching through her bag.

"I am dealing with a fucking crisis here and my mother has disowned me and" She trails off and throws her purse on the counter and a few items fall out. A tampon, a contacts case and some sunglasses.

"I can't find my damn wallet" she says as she throws things out of her purse. In seconds she has a pile of stuff on the countertop. Steve looks at her wide eyed in disbelief. A man walks up to him and whispers

"If there is a card linked just charge it and let her go, people are staring."

She finally finds her wallet at the bottom of the bag. When she looks up, she is slightly surprised to see another man present.

He catches her eyes widening slightly and smiles wide "Hello ma'am I am the manager, John" he nods his head, scowls at Steve and retreats from the front desk.

She picks the wallet up and turns it upside down. She slumps and sobs. She wipes her face with the back of her sleeve.

"Sir, I do not know where my ID is, I'm sorry." The man behind the counter looking at her with a mixture of shock and pity says "Ma'am state your full name?"

"Jane Miriam Stoneybrooke," he glances at the computer screen and back to Sandra "and your date of birth please," "September 16th, 1971."

The man glances at the computer again and clicks a few buttons "you're all set ma'am, have a pleasant day."

Sandra exhaled and picked up her items and threw them in her purse. She heads down the street near the boutique stores that are arranged in a circle with the parking garage on the inside.

She picks up her phone, scrolls to a contact name Isaiah "Mike" Finiter.

She Says "Hello" into the phone in her Boston accent "Mike man, where is my stuff I needed yesterday. Times up I'm on my way" she hangs up the phone and heads into the parking garage.

She walks along the cars until she finds a white Lexus.

She tries the handle and looks inside but it's a car with a key hole not a button start. She continues looking and comes across a black Mercedes.

When she peeks inside, it is a button start. She tries the driver door, and it's locked.

She tries the back-passenger side door, which is open. She notices a car seat in the back seat.

The middle console is down and there are wrappers all over the sticky cup holders. "Ding ding" she says and leans over in the car to push the button to open the other doors in the car.

She gets in the driver side and checks the glove box "No key" she says puzzled. She looks around the car thinking where else would a key be hidden. Some cars have an alarm that goes off if you pushed the start button without a key being near.

She then looks in the middle console. She smiles and closes the top; she leaves it there and pushes the brake and the start button.

Sandra pulls up to 0818 Chestnut place and sees Jake standing there with a blue Camry, a petite blonde lady and a nervous look on his face.

Her French accent returns "Smith honey, sorry I'm late," she comes and kisses him quickly on both cheeks "I had to go back to the hotel for my wallet and then to the store to get my bottle of wine" she smiles at the lady and kisses her twice, once on each cheek.

"You must be Veronica, Oui?" Veronica looks taken aback by the kissing and takes a few steps back.

"Uh, yes ma'am I'm Veronica Standberry, the Realtor. Sorry

if this appears rude, but I didn't know Miriam had a daughter."

Veronica says with a nervous laugh. Sandra walks towards the house "yes, ma mère wanted me to have a normal life, not the life of an heir," she said waving her hands in the air dramatically as she spoke.

"She came to the United States, and I stayed in France. Mother just became the director of her hungry children's charity, which requires her to stay in France."

She makes it to the door and turns to face the two of them "Long story short mère and I cannot be on the same continent so she is in France and my Smith and I are here. I'm selling the house so the sale of this one is contingent on the sale of my house back home Oui?"

"Yes, Ms. Stoneybrooke uhh, er Mrs." Veronica stumbled on what to call Sandra. Jake jumped in "She kept her maiden name" he shrugged smile widely "there goes a modern-day woman for ya" he said with a chuckle and the worst French accent Sandra had ever heard. *Mental note to self,* Sandra thought, work *on Jake's French accent.*

Veronica smiled and opened the door to the house. She began her script on what to say, what to point out and points to make as they walked through the house.

Sandra whispered while keeping her head straightforward, "your French accent is terrible." Jake scoffs and rolls his eyes, "Well a heads up that we would be French would have helped. I spoke to you literally 20 minutes ago."

"Huh" Veronica slowed and turned around.

"Oh, nothing" Sandra said widening her eyes and looking around the house

"This reminds me of my home back in France,"

She looks at Jake "honey, we just have to have it." Veronica smiles and pulls out a blue folder "I can just leave you guys for a few minutes with the information for you guys to talk it over." With that, she walks out of the room. Sandra stares after her "Oh what I wouldn't do to be 20 something and perky again." Jake rolls his eyes, "please you're only like 35. Anyway, how the hell am I supposed to sign paperwork, you left me in the dark?"

Sandra dug around in her purse and pulled out an ID and a passport. She handed it to him and watched him look it over.

"Oh, I took your last name huh?" He smirks and looks up at her. Damn that smile she thought as her eyes narrowed her eyes.

"I'm a spoiled long-lost heiress, you live to please me. Anyway, Mike set our accounts up," She whispered "and transferred my money into, well, some of my money. It's a joint account so you have access too."

She pulled out the Id she had made for herself and placed it on the blue folder. "Oh, so when we get caught, I'll go down with you, huh?"

She snorted, "have I ever gotten caught?" Before he could respond Veronica walked back into the room. "So, guys, what do you think?" She said smiling at the two of them with her arms stretched out.

"We have a deal," they said in unison.

Veronica shook Sandra off and gestured for them to move to the table. There she explained and highlighted everything, and then they signed on the dotted line. "Can I see your ID please?" Veronica asks. They handed over their identification and Veronica left the room with "hold on a sec" and a raised finger. When she returned, she has copies of the ID's and gives them back the originals.

Veronica led them to the front door, "I can get your keys by the end of business. So how about I meet you guys here in the morning for the exchange?"

Sandra jumps in "No that's okay. I will come by your office to get it." She says as she grabs her hands and says their goodbyes. Jake walks Sandra to her car and waits until Veronica drives off.

They stop at the Mercedes, "Okay, when did you get this?" Jake says as he gestures with his hands over the top of the car.

"Where I got it isn't important. I will get a new one today. With access to my accounts, it's finally time to make myself at home." She says with a smile as she opens the door to get in.

Jake holds the top of the car door and looks down at her. As she looked up at him the glint of the sun sprinkled into her eyes. She turns towards her bag, that she put on the passenger side seat, and pulls out her Michael Kors sunglasses. She turns her attention back towards Jake.

"What are you going to do with the car?" he asks. She looks around him towards his Camry.

"You want it? It's way better than that piece of junk you're driving."

He holds his hands up in a surrendering motion, "hey leave my car alone, it's mine and it's legal."

She smiled "Next time you see me mine will be to, well legal to Jane Stoneybrooke at least she said with a wink."

He chuckles, and she slips her sunglasses into place. He closes the car door. She puts her seatbelt on and heads off, back to the outlet mall.

Sandra drives off the lot with a 2015 ford focus paid in full and headed to the dmv for proper registration. After 2 excruciating hours waiting in lines, just for a 7-minute encounter with the clerk it was too late for lunch but too early for dinner. *What should one do at 1:30 pm?*

She thought to herself. Well, she needed to find Slickey; she knew that for sure. She also needed to find a place to rent furniture. At the next red light, she grabbed her phone and opened her Samsung notes. She started typing what she had to do:

- Find Slickey
  - Set up a bank account for my niece's college fund to be transferred to
  - Investigate new neighborhood
  - Exit plan?

She purposely kept everything vague and used unique languages. Can't have big brother catching on. Then she created a separate page and made her list

- Order house furniture to rent - entire rooms or designer?
  - Tomorrows BBQ last chance to get invited to weekly poker night
  - Shop for myself and Smith for BBQ, rich first impression.

The light turned green, and she threw her phone into the passenger seat. She needed to find another hotel, her last one, before she drove back into the city.

When she got settled into the New Life Hotel, she got her computer out and did more checking for hacker's heist on the internet.

Slickey is good, and she always went big. Sandra ordered door dash some chicken Alfredo from a place that was close and spent the night working out her plan.

#

Later that night Sandra walked into a bar she found a few blocks from her hotel. She walks in noting the dark lighting everywhere except to the dance floor, which was lit up with multi-colored flashing lights.

She made her way to the bar, DJ playing a mixture between top 40 and classic hip hop music. She sits on a vacant bar stool and waits for the redhead behind the bar to notice her.

She pulled out her phone to look at some reviews of this place. While she was at it, she checked her alerts to see if she had any hits on Slickey.

She looked up from her phone and glanced down at where the bartender was. The best red could never come out of a bottle, she thought as she looked at the fire red hair of the bartender.

The girl finally realizes she has a customer besides the big rock looking guy she was talking to and heads over.

"Hey Hun, what can I get you?" She says smacking a piece of gum loudly as Sandra hears a slight southern drawl.

Sandra contemplates whether to be Jane and go French or fall into her comfortable Boston.

She smiles at the bartender. "What do you have fruity doll?" she asks thick Boston coming through. The bartender looks up to the left, as if thinking, and then nods at herself.

"I've got just the thing" she said and then headed back to mix her concoction.

Sandra is babysitting her drink when a guy with brown hair, short to his scalp and piercing blue eyes walks up and sits next to her.

Looking at him makes her think mental note: buy contacts Jane has hazel eyes. She turns towards him and lets her legs swing down off the bar stool, swiping against him. She notices him stiffen and moves his legs back slightly.

Hmm, weird, she thinks to herself. She looks at him more clearly and sees he is eyeing her out of his peripheral. She swivels in the chair to check her surroundings. She sees people on the dance floor dancing.

There is a couple in a booth in the corner practically having sex. There is a line for the ladies' bathroom. She sees one blonde sneak into the men's room with 2 of her girls standing guard at the door.

There is a pool game going on with a group of guys. She stares for a moment while one has his turn. He sucks, she thinks with a chuckle. She is content with her scan of the room and returned to her drink.

She turns herself back around in her chair and returns to her drink. She notices it is slightly more to the left than she left it. She holds on to the glass and looks around the room, slowly bringing it to her mouth like she is getting ready to drink.

She notices the guy next to her has not left but has not made a move to flirt or even talk to her. Everything in the room looks just as it did when she looked the last time, besides her drink.

She put the glass to her lips and tipped it, careful to keep her lips closed around the rim... She feels the liquid touch her lips, and she puts the glass down. She quickly takes a napkin and dabs her lips dry.

She turns her attention back to the guy sitting next to her and the bartender catches her attention. When they lock eyes, the bartender quickly looks away as if she was never watching her. Hmm, Sandra thinks, the guy and the bartender?

Sandra is getting ready to say something when a girl with a high-pitched voice says, "Oh my god! Is that you, honey?"

Sandra turns around and sees Slickey. She is flooded with

relief and audibly exhales. She pushes the drink toward the bartender and places a $20 on the counter. She gets up and goes over to her and leans in for a hug.

"Slickey thank god, I've been trying to find you" she whispers in her ear in her natural southern drawl.

"I know, my computer has been giving me hits of people looking me up. I don't know what to call you, who are you today?"

Sandra releases the hug and smiles at her, she exclaims in her Boston accent "Hey girl, it's been too long."

Slickey looks at her and smiles "Gigi girl, let's get out of here." The two girls turn towards the door and head out of the bar. "My cars down here" Slickey points.

"I walked, my hotel is nearby" Sandra says and the ladies' turn and walk towards Slickey's car. Sandra tilts her head slowly to the right and hears a set of footsteps walking behind her. She takes Slickey hands and spins her in a circle while hysterically laughing. Slickey catches on and joins in on the laughter.

The two ladies stumble a bit and Slickey says "Just like old times, I missed you girl" and then they continued to walk towards the car at a faster pace. Slickey leans in and whispers "who's the guy" Slickey asks "I don't know, acting creepy at the bar" before they reach the car and quickly jump in.

Once they get in Slickey locks the door. Before she can ask Sandra anything there is a tap at the window and the bar guy holds up a credit card with a smile "You left this" he says. Slickey looks at her with one eyebrow raised "don't open the window, just pull off" Sandra says "I have a nasty feeling." Slickey put the key in the ignition and pulled off.

"What the hell was that about?" Slickey asked while alternating between the road and Sandra.

"I really don't know, I think-" Sandra shakes her head "just a nasty feeling."

Slickey nods and asks "so searching me up huh?" Sandra seems to relax a fraction bit, audibly exhaling a breath.

"I have a job in a little over four weeks and need a hacker, you in?"

Slickey raises one eyebrow and makes a left turn, "Yea, I'm in," she says.

Chapter Eight
Flashback, Trapped

Basement

I open the door to the basement. It creaks a little so I make sure I open it slow so the sound echoes in the gloomy space. I descend the stairs taking them one at time stomping my foot louder than necessary, increasing the noise the lower I get. Taking my time, going slowly, watching her slumped body go rigid. Watching as she sits up straight and whimpers. As I reach the bottom of the stairs, she is sobbing. I grin the Grinch's grin as I watch and soak in the fear, let it seep into pores and energize my soul.

The ground, the concrete floor is hard and cold. I have been laying on it so long my body is numb. The corner of the room against the wall is wet. I have to lie in it because my chain doesn't stretch far enough. My chain, I have a chain around my neck, like a dog. Why has this happened to me, to my life? Will I die here? I can't get too far into my hopelessness because I hear the door creek. I go rigid. It's him, he's coming back. I sit up as I hear him coming down the stairs. Don't cry, don't cry, I tell myself, but it doesn't work. The already loud sound of his boots hitting the steps bangs like a building being demolished and echo as he gets closer. Suddenly the footsteps stopped and I sob.

"Please" she says "just let me go". Ha! Let her go. Why would I do that? She was a fighter, took me using the stun gun for her to go down. All that work I had to do, oh I will enjoy my prize "Hello Jelena."

She stiffens and sniffles. "Y yess. Please, please let me go. I just want to see my family again please." I chuckle, "Your family? You have no kids' silly girl."

She stiffens, "Why am I here?" she asks "What do you want?"

I walk towards her, dragging my feet along. I stop at the work table just out of her reach and pick up a 6-inch knife.

I continue towards her "I have a friend who thinks you're getting in the way and you need to be eliminated."

I watched as she inhaled sharply, her eyes darted from one side to the other. "No need to think my dear, you don't know who he is or why you're getting in the way. All you know is that you need to be eliminated and I will have a hell of a time eliminating you."

I walk closer until I'm standing so close my leg is touching her. I see her straining her neck with her head bouncing back and forth trying to hear.

She tries to slide back and hits the wall. Her momentum knocked the wind out of her. I see fear in her eyes as my silhouette comes into focus for her. Her eyes dart up and down adjusting she makes out my mask, her eyes dart down to my hands where I have black gloves.

Good girl, trying to get any details she can. "Sorry, all covered up, I told you I wouldn't underestimate you again. I kept my word."

I bend down and take the knife I had in my boot and scrape it across her arm. She jerks away and is halted by her dumb decision and hits the wall hard again.

She screams, and I watch the blood drip down her arm. It splatters because she jerked it away from the blade.

I take a step closer, putting one leg on the right side of her and the other on the left side, blocking her in, and putting a brief pressure on each side of her. Her eyes are wide with terror and she thrashes around.

I step in closer and tighten my hold. Her legs kick to no avail, and she punches me. "Yes Jelena, fight" I groan with pleasure right as she punches me in the groin. Then I see red.

He reels back in pain, and I hear the clank of the knife falling to the ground. My eyes track where it is and I try to calculate the distance and whether I can get to it. He kicks the knife to the other side of the room while he takes a deep breath and straightens himself. "What a bad girl," he said, growling.

I see him walk over to the wall and crank a lever and I suspend into the air. My eyes go wide with horror and I grab at the chain around my neck as I'm lifted off the ground. He stops so only my tip toes touch the ground. I try to keep my feet on the ground to relieve the pressure on my neck. I take shallow breaths quickly.

I try to slow down my breathing, but I am panicking. "Naughty girls get punished Jelena." He says in a singsong tone. I watch as he turns a lamp on and pulls a curtain back off the wall. I didn't even know it was there. I suddenly gasped as I saw 5 bodies of women all suspended from the ceiling like me, but these women were dead.

Their eyes are wide open and I know I am feeling the horror they felt right before they were killed. Will I be next, dead like them? There is one girl whose arms are still grasping the chain around her neck. "Please no, please, I'm sorry I won't do it again" I choke out. "Oh, I know you won't" He smirks and walks over to me and *begins cutting my clothes off. I sobbed "Please no" I half whisper half cough.*

I spend all my effort trying to keep my toes on the ground so I don't choke. I can't do anything to fight back. I sob silently as I close my eyes and become numb as I am poked, prodded and violated.

Angry Zumba

Present

Dan is in the kitchen cutting up vegetables as Jelena opens the front door. He listens as her keys drop and the clank of her heels as she kicks them off before she gets onto the carpet. She walks and then stops. Must be checking the mail, he thinks to himself.

He puts the carrots he just finished cutting in the pot next to him on the stove. He bends down, checking the oven as Jelena walks into the kitchen. She hovers over the pot, looking in. "Mmmm" she says "this smells good." They lean in and kiss each other.

"How was your day?" Jelena asks Dan as she grabs plates and silverware to go make the table.

"Working on this project, a building that the client wants is specific. He keeps on having me change this and that because it doesn't fit his 'vision'" he says using air quotes. She giggles and walks into the living room, "Oh the life of an architect." she yells from the other room.

Dan finishes the food without trying to have further conversation with his wife. He brings the food over to the island and sets it down.

"Dinner Jelena" he says as he walks over to the pantry and

opens a wine cooler stationed in the corner and grabs the wine. They both sit at the island and bow their heads as they say a silent prayer.

They eat "Mmm honey this is muy deliciosa" <very good> she says with a full mouth. Dan scowls and takes his first fork full of food. "So, how did your day go?" Dan asks.

"My students are working on a case," she says. She looked up to the right, thinking of how much to say. "We started at the beginning of this week. Tomorrow we will come together and see where each group is at and see if anyone needs my guidance or is close to solving it."

Dan takes another bite studying her closely "Geesh Jelena give your kids a break" he jokes "It is only Tuesday" they both laugh in between bites.

"So, honey," Jelena begins, "Angela wants to have a girl's night this weekend, so we were thinking Saturday night, does that work for you?"

"I have nothing planned so yea its works," Dan says "maybe I could join you two?"

Jelena snorts, "It's called girl's night not to make my friend feel like a third wheel night."

Dan exhales slightly with a sound sounding half like a laugh and half like a growl.

"Yea, I'll call up my brothers. Or maybe I will just sit at home and relax," he says with a shrug.

"Yes, go with your brothers," Jelena urges "just don't go to Club Space, because that's where we'll be."

Dan looks at her "Club Space, where is that at?"

Jelena looks at him suspiciously, "where is it? It's a few minutes away from downtown," she says.

"Okay but where," Dan urges.

Jelena picked up her glass of wine to drink and looked at Dan over the rim of the glass. "What are you asking?" she said.

Dan looks at her through squinting eyes and then shakes his head "nothing, forget It." he said and continues eating.

They finish up dinner with conversation about upcoming movies to see how things are tense at work between Jelena and the other supervisory Special Agent Romanary, debating on the issues in politics and whether The View is an excellent source of information. They cleared their plates, laughing about whether they should take political advice from Whoopi Goldberg. Jelena heads upstairs. "Wait," Dan says, "I thought we find something to stream tonight."

"Sure honey," she said, "but it's Wednesday. You know I do Zumba at 7:00 pm on Wednesday's."

"Can I go?" Dan asks her as he shifts his weight from one foot to the next.

Jelena turns fully to face him. "Daniel Cohert, I've been trying to get you to go to Zumba with me for 2 years and you always say no puedo hacer esos bailes Latinos" <I can't do those Latin dances> Jelena says as she does an interpretation of Dan trying to salsa and other moves that involve him moving his hips.

Dan breaks out in laughter so hard he has to hold on to the wall for support. "I do not dance like that," Dan says in between breaths.

Jelena walks over to him and loops her arm into his "Sure you can come; the class can use the amusement" she says as they walk towards the stairs together.

"And whatever you said in Spanish, I will assume it was 'Dan your dancing skills are the best' and I would love you in my class."

Jelena lets out a loud snort "Yea okay, that's what I said."

They get to the top of the stairs and Dan stops and turns towards her "Jelena, ya' know how I hate when you talk so I can't understand."

Jelena stops and turns towards her husband, fully facing him with her hands on her hips and her eyebrows raised "you knew when we dated that I would not suppress my culture for you. How have your Spanish lessons been going? Because Señora Jones has been texting me asking where you are. So instead of standing there telling me how much you cannot understand me stop procrastinating and take the time to show you care about learning and knowing your wife's culture. "Parce que j'ai pris le temps" <because I took the time> She says in French, then she turns on her heels into the bedroom.

Dan looks on irritated that she threw this big fit his as he watches her grab clothes and head towards the guest bedroom "ready in 10" she says barely a whisper as she hurries past without making eye contact. Making sure he could say nothing in return with a slam of the door.

Dan goes into the master bedroom and calls his older brother. "Hey Drew" he says as his brother picks up the phone

"What's up bro, how's everything going?"

"Jelena just went postal on me for no good reason,"

"Alright let me hear it,"

"We were talking about Zumba and she said something in Spanish. There is nothing wrong with me needing to understand what she's saying and I told her that."

"Little brother, you have been married for 15 years, you should've known what she said. If you would have said the same thing in French, she would've known what you said, because she took the time to learn our language."

Dan heard the door to the guest room opening, "I have to go; she's leaving and I'm going with her." Dan hangs the phone up and puts it in his pocket, he quickly puts on some shorts and runs to the door. He gets to the front porch just as Jelena is getting in her car. He shuts the front door, turns to lock it and then hustle to her passenger door. She rolls down the window and says "It's at the yoga studio by Harris Teeter around the corner" she shuts her window and she drives off.

Dan gets to the studio and everyone is already dancing, he falls in the back. Jelena is up front with Angela and two other men, Angela spots him in the mirror and diverts her eyes. "Chica, Dan esta aqui?" <Girl, Dan is here> as she looks up into the mirror again.

Dan gave a half smile and wave and got an icy stare in return as she focused back on the instructor. Dan struggled in the back of the class, really struggled. He watched on as Jelena, Angela and those two guys barely broke a sweat laughing the entire time, looking like they were having a grand time.

He watched on in envious rage. Why am I so mad? Dan thought to himself, why does seeing her laugh make me mad? Dan continued to focus on his wife, and not on the instructor which he should have been because he was working his ass off to look like he was keeping up. Because she's laughing without me, he thinks as he loses his footing and falls right on his ass, in front of the entire class.

The class looks at him through the mirror and then everyone turns around as if to get a good look.

At the end of the class, Jelena and her friends walked over to their bags and grabbed water bottles.

They talked and drank as Dan walked up. "Hola Dan" Angela says, and then as if she noticed her mistake she said "Hey Dan what's up?"

Dan groaned why she can't keep our business our business, he thought. He smiled and patted Angela on the shoulder, "Hey, Angela."

He turns and looks at the two guys sticking his hand out he says "I don't think I have had the privilege, I'm Dan" Belle shook his hand first "I'm Jared Belle and this my older brother Chad." Bell reaches and shakes Dan's hand "and we know who you are" Bell says "we work with Cohert" he said nonchalantly.

Dan gets immediately defensive. "Just because you work with her means you know who I am?"

"We are on her team," Bell attempts to reiterate "We know she has a husband named Dan. We spend a lot of time together, the least we could do is to know if each other are married or not."

Dan speaks but Jelena rolls her eyes "Okay guys I'll see ya later." Jelena turns towards Angela "Angela it's a go for Club Space this weekend."

The ladies hug, and everyone goes about their ways. Jelena and Dan walk back to the parking lot in silence, nervously Dan says, "I need to come to more classes. Never thought it would be so much work." His attempt at a conversation is ignored. He watches Jelena spot her car and go to walk off.

He grabs her arm "Jelena wait" but she slips through his grip and goes to her car. He stands there and watches her plug in her phone and begins blasting Jennifer Lopez's Dinero as she speeds away.

Jelena drives home blasting Dinero by J-Lo singing "Yo quiero, yo quiero dinero, ay Yo quiero, yo quiero dinero, ay I just want the green, want the money, want the cash flow Yo quiero la venta, sí, sin cuenta, sí, lo siento," she sings at the top of her lungs.

The song goes off and she turns the music down a bit as an old song by Usher plays in the background. About 4 songs later, Jelena pulls into her driveway.

I could have been home earlier, she thought, but she took the scenic route. She walks into the house and takes off her shoes at the door. She doesn't spot Dan downstairs, so she walks into the kitchen and makes herself a cup of hot chocolate with a little caramel cream mixed in.

She sits down on the couch and turns on the TV to catch up on Good Bones reruns. She finished her drink and must have fallen asleep because when she looked at the clock 2 hours had passed.

She walked into the kitchen and dumped her cup in the sink, not bothering to put it in the dishwasher, and went upstairs to take a shower.

When she made it to the bedroom and noticed that Dan had his sketchbooks and notebooks displayed all across the bed. He was so heavily into his project he hardly noticed her come in; she attempted to creep past him.

"Jelena wait" he said as he put his pencil down and looked up "can we talk, please." She sighed heavily and rolled her eyes. She sat on the edge of the bed, forcing him to get up and stand in front of her if he wanted to see her face. He followed suit and got off the bed, standing in front of her.

He tried to step closer, but she locked her knees shut, not allowing him to. "I'm sorry about the insensitive comment about not being able to understand you" he looked at her waiting for a response, or any acknowledgment at all. She takes a deep breath and looks at him,

"You need to know my language; I know your language as

we discussed when we were dating a decade ago. There is no excuse for you not to know my language and as a result feel emasculated, disrespected, isolated or whatever it is you feel when I speak in Spanish. The reason you cannot understand what I am saying has nothing to do with me."

He takes a deep breath and tries to take a step forward, she tenses and locks her knees again, *and this will not just go away* she thinks to herself.

Confía en tus instintos mi hija, trust your instinct, my daughter as her grandmother used to say as she took her hand and pressed it against Jelena's stomach. Jelena shook off her little tangent and looked up at Dan.

"I know," he begins "It is not fair that you have held up your end of the bargain and I have not."

She sticks up her hand in a stop motion "No" she starts sternly "it's not fair that I cared enough about my husband to know and learn about his culture and he did not offer me that same respect" she says as she gets up, forcing him to take a few steps back. She goes into the bathroom and closes the door. Dan sits on the bed and slumps when he hears the click of the locks.

Jelena turns the shower water on and sits on the toilet. She puts her head in her hands and takes a deep breath. Aliento <breath> Jelena. Why is my gut telling me that something is wrong? Jelena always trusted her instincts and in leading a life as an FBI agent her instincts have rarely done her wrong.

Jelena hears her Abuelita as clear as day 'Eres una chica fuerte mi hija. No confíes en nadie excepto en ti mismo y confía en tus instintos', "I am a strong girl, rely on no one and trust my instincts" Jelena whispers the translation as she cries. "Abuelita" she whispers, "He recorrido un largo camino. Pensé que superé mi pasado" but deep down she knew her pasado, past, is not something she could ever overcome.

Jelena got into the shower and stood under the water and let the falling drops hit her, willing it to wash all her problems away. She didn't know how long she sat on the toilet but she did not want to run into Dan so she stayed in the shower extra-long. And when she was done, she cleaned the tub and made bath water. Jelena sat in the water until she was nearly sleeping before she pulled herself out. She slowly dried off and put her robe on. Jelena creaked open the door and went across the room the closets. She entered the closet where she put a tank and some shorts on and went directly to the bed, rolled over and dozed off.

\#

When Dan woke up Jelena wasn't there. She left the house without a sound or a word.

Dan did his morning routine and went downstairs to get his notebook.

August 8th, 2018

I upset Jelena because I do not know Spanish. She has always had a flare for the dramatics. I went to Zumba with her and she had friends there. Who knew she had any friends besides Angela? I don't like the vibe I was getting from that guy. He was too overprotective to be a co-worker/friend. We haven't done the folder routine this morning. Hell, she was gone before I got up. Guess she forgot she had to hand back fake graded papers. I will follow her one day soon. Or maybe I should turn her in? Turn her into where, huh? She works for the FBI!

Dan gets up to go shower and then goes down to the kitchen

for a bowl of oatmeal. He finishes with about 10 minutes left before he has to leave the house to go to work. He spends this time in the office searching through Jelena's files and drawers. Dan freezes when he thinks he hears a car in his driveway. He hurriedly stuffs things back to where they need to be and run to the front door to look out of the peephole. Nothing, he thinks.

Dan sits on the bench next to the front door. "What am I doing" he rubs his hand through his hair "What do I want to find? Why am I snooping like I haven't been with this girl for almost 2 decades?" staring absently down the hall in the office's direction.

Chapter Ten

Break it down

Jelena woke up early to make sure she left before Dan got up. She drove around the corner and switched cars and then headed to HQ. When Jelena arrived Boss was inside his car on the phone. He appeared to be arguing with someone, so Jelena did not wait for me. After taking a few steps, she heard "Cohert" in a gruff voice. Jelena stopped and turned around to face her Boss. When we caught up to her, he didn't say a word, didn't even stop. She gave him a puzzled look and then followed him. He has the courtesy to wait for me at the door, she thought sarcastically. Everyone gathered around once they heard the door open. Jelena walks to the kitchen table where she sees her team plus Captain Cross. "Hello, everyone this is our Supervisory Special Agent, he is supervising the FBI part of the team" Jelena gestures to Captain Cross "Boss this is Captain Cross of MDPD."

The two men shook hands and provided pleasantries. Boss took a seat at the table and looked at Cohert "break it down" he said getting right down to business. Cohert took a step back as she said "past crimes team go". Clearweather and Jonathan stood up and Clearweather began "If you all would look to your tablets, I have shared a file" Cohert took her tablet and handed it to the Boss. Cross looked over Belle's shoulder. Clearweather looked around the room to make sure it accommodated everyone and then continued, "1st we have Highworth in 2000 with her mall scheme." Clearweather described the con and the evidence they had against her. "In 2005 we have her at an investment firm" He continues and again he described the scheme and told about the little evidence they had in this case. "Where is the paper trail?" the Boss asked.

Clearweather shifted his eyes back and forth, "Uh sir, we uh have a paper trail for Gloria Givworthings. She hacked the University's system and input herself into the system, not knowing a tech at the school realized that there was a breach. The tech found the name and erased it after notifying his supervisor. This is how the firm caught that Gloria er Highworth never went to school. We have a trail of Gloria transferring small amounts at first and then one enormous sum of money into an account at an offshore bank. The only evidence we have that ties Gloria to Highworth is seeing Highworth on various cameras throughout the firm."

Cross spoke up "what about the office Highworth used, do we not have any evidence that ties Highworth to Gloria's office?"

Clearweather cleared his throat, "the cleaning crew came and got to the office before the crime scene techs had the chance."

The Boss sighed heavily, "so the only thing we have tying Gloria to Highworth is seeing Highworth in the same building where Gloria was said to have been employed. Can we tie her to the office or just the building?"

"There are only cameras on the common floors open to the public sir" Clearweather said. Cross cleared his throat, "okay what do we have after 2005? Jonathan stood up and swiped over his tablet, "from 2005 to 2015 we have five men who died of what the corners report states as natural causes. Each of these men were married to Sandra Highworth without an alias. She would marry quickly, take out a life insurance policy and wait two years for it to mature than her husband would die of natural causes."

"Why did the coroner's office or the local PD not catch on to this," asked Cross.

"Because she would cross state lines. This allowed her to use her actual name and not be suspected."

"Okay, so why haven't we brought charges for this on her?" Boss said. This time Cohert spoke up

"Because the corner office in all 5 cases said the men died of natural causes, even though they were healthy 40 or 50 something year olds. At the time we could get none of the families to agree to have the body exhumed."

Boss said, "well try again now. Go get the paperwork pushed through four exhumations. Once everything is written up, I'll try to push it through." Jonathan looked at Belle and nodded, who stood up and continued

"Which brings us to 2016 when a gallery in California reported that their whole exhibit had been replaced with fakes. The report specified a detective coming on when the alarm went off. They attempted to steal a piece under heavy surveillance. Once the thieves broke the glass, the vault door shut and locked them in. Detective Worthy aka Highworth came to apprehend the thieves and collect evidence. She was left alone to work and then left approximately an hour later. It wasn't until a few days after when the gallery owner tried to sell a piece he found out not only one but his whole exhibit was fakes."

Jonathan looked around to see if there were any interjections, then he continued, "We have Highworth on camera in the gallery falsely portraying herself as a detective. We have handwriting experts' confirmations of Highworth's signature on some evidence bags as detective Linda Worthy. There was a detective, Linda Worthy, but she was out on maternity leave."

Belle looked around the room and spotted Clearweather glaring, Cross spoke up "I remember hearing about this, the media and all the reports I've read said there was no suspect."

"Right," Clearweather spoke up "there was no evidence tying Highworth to the stolen items," he said scowling.

"I had to do some serious work," Belle explained. "Looking at the camera's facial recognition would confirm with an 86% certainty that the lady in the video was Highworth. On a whim I asked for a handwriting analysis because everyone at the local PD was telling me it had to be Linda snooping around a big case, no one even bothered to ask Linda because the evidence ended up in the evidence locker for the attempted theft."

Clearweather stood up speaking loudly "and then," and all eyes turned towards him, "we have the jewelry heist of 2017," he continued lowering his voice level as the sentence progressed. "The grand ball was an invitation only event. The guest list was electronic so she easily could have added herself on the list. We got a hold of the list and there is a Sandra Highworth on the list."

"Actual name again," Cross said.

"Yes sir," Clearweather said, giving his boss eye contact. "Most of the guests had jewelry missing, off of their bodies." He said with emphasis.

"Sounds like a classic case of pick pocketing," Boss said, "is there any evidence of a partner?" he asked.

"There was a Jake Blaten present at the ball, he and Highworth are the only ones who were there alone. He got thrown out for getting caught looking into a lady's purse. They searched him on the way out and had nothing on him besides his wallet and car keys. Shortly after the guest started realizing their jewelry was missing, Jake was suspected but then cleared when security told the police they searched him before they let him go. Highworth was gone and did not get caught up in the sweep," Clearweather finished.

"Where there any cameras?" Cross asked.

"No," Clearweather said "the rich and famous love their privacy."

Cross began, "So how do we know she is the one who did it?"

Cohert jumped in, "I have discovered that Highworth has three bank accounts all offshore. I got a friend to tell me off the record that these three accounts have approximately four million dollars in it." Cross looked at her sharply, "Why off the record?"

"Because each of these offshore accounts has strict policies in place that prevent the FBI or any international law enforcement to get access to their client's information. So, the manager gave me what he could legally on the record and the rest off the record."

Cross glared "so we got the information illegally," he accused.

"No," she said sharply, "Sandra Highworth has 3 offshore accounts under her name. She knows the law and knows we can't touch them so she doesn't care about hiding or secrecy." She looked at him waiting for him to speak again, when he didn't, she continued

"As I was saying, Highworth has three accounts. After the jewelry heist we found four different buyers who had bought individual pieces of diamonds. Since the buyers were planning on legally selling these pieces, the serial numbers had to be registered. At the time that the buyers registered the serial numbers, Highworth had four deposits into her offshore account."

"If the banks cannot give us the information, how do you know, another off the record?" Cross asked sarcastically

"The banks confirmed the date and time of the deposits but would not confirm the amount, or the account balance, or even which client's account. They confirmed Highworth has an account there. We don't have enough to hold up in court, but we have enough to connect the dots."

Clearweather jumped back in "since the sale was illegal the buyers got arrested and did not get their money back and since the jewelry was in pieces, the owners got reimbursed by their insurance. All four of the buyers identified Highworth as their seller, but the money was not located and there was no record of a sell since it was illegal."

Cohert said, "I can tie all the mentioned heists to one of the three accounts by taking the approximate dates and asking the manager if there was a deposit made during this time. Once we arrest her and get full access, we will have the confirmation."

Boss looked at Cohert and said, "That's all we got?" Cohert looked around the table at her team. When no one jumped in she replied "yes sir, now time for the current crime. Rodriguez"

"Hold on" Boss said "some of these cases are circumstantial. We need physical evidence."

"Yes sir," Cohert said "when our system was wiped we lost a lot of data. Most of the information we had on Highworth had an electronic element. I had all the hard copies we had in the archives copied back into the system for easy access, but everything we had was not there." Boss sat there silently, obviously a sign to move on, she thought. Rodriguez, she said again.

Rodriguez got up "esta bien chicos," she said cheerfully "the auction is on September 8th. I have access to the list and there were two people added to this yesterday, and right now the list has not been changed. If Highworth wants in on the auction she has to get on this list. The company doing the auction is Jones & Johnson. I called and asked their policy. They complete the guest list 1 month before the auction. I identified myself and found out that the guest list for Danielle Price's auction has been complete for 2 weeks, there has been no talk of having anyone added."

Boss said, "So knowing that Highworth got into Miami at the beginning of the week, we have to think she has some plan in motion to get in the auction. Can she hack herself into the auction?"

"Yes sir, she could but she would have to be at the auction to steal the money."

Cohert spoke up, "Our tech guy is keeping track of Highworth through the recognition. We found her at rent a room and got the name on the receipts. Highworth is going by Jane Stoneybrooke."

Rodriguez continued, "we also have Mrs. Stoneybrooke making major purchases around the city. She has rented furniture from Rent a Room; she has a house under contract and has bought a car."

Cross interrupted, "I find it hard to believe she bought a house."

"Per the Realtors office, a Mr. and Mrs. Stoneybrooke have signed for a house in Sunny Isles Beach. No money has changed hands yet because the Realtor said the deal is contingent on a house being sold in France. They have 30 days. Since the house was empty and Stoneybrooke is such a prominent name, it allowed them to move in after they signed the paperwork.

She signed yesterday. Move in date is technically today, but the realtor said she got the keys early yesterday evening and called Stoneybrooke and asked if they would like the keys early and they agreed. She has been moving things in since yesterday evening. Veronica, the relator, mentioned having a hard time finding her Realtor in France and that this was making things slow on her side.

Cohert spoke up "Sunny Isles Beach, do we know where the house is?"

Rodriguez saw a glimpse of an emotion in her eyes, but I went for it before she could identify it. "Sí Chica, it's a cul-de-sac neighborhood called The Pines. They are staying at 0818 Chestnut place." Rodriguez looks at her friend understanding Cohert lived i the same neighborhood.

"Okay," Cohert clears her throat "Continue."

Rodriguez swipes over on her tablet. "Okay, if I was going to steal all these people's money, this is how I would do it. First, I need to be invited to the auction. They have completed this step, assuming that Sandra Highworth is Jane Stoneybrooke. Next, I would have to find someone who could hack into Jones & Johnson's system. This is how it works." Rodriguez put the tablet down and took a half step back. "During the auction the 1st piece is bid on. The winner then wires that amount of money into an account, they give the number to them as they win the bid. All the money at the end of the night gets put through some transfer system and goes into an account owned by the client, minus Jones & Johnson's fee, before Jones & Johnson leaves for the night. According to the auction company, this

Happy Hour

Jelena got into her car and pulled out her Samsung notes. She had to go grocery shopping, and she needed to go get ink and paper for her at home printer and would like to hit Barnes & Noble for something new. She decided she would go home and hit the spots closer to her neighborhood, which meant she had to go to the other house and change cars.

On her way she would drive past 0818 Chestnut and look and see if Ms. Sandra Highworth is in her backyard. She changed cars before she drove past in case Highworth recognized a government vehicle and it would out her. She drove through the winding streets looking for her destination. That's one thing she hated about cul de sacs was the winding streets. She approached Chestnut and started looking at the mailboxes for house numbers. She spotted 0818 and did a quick inventory of the house. As she was passing, she saw her, Highworth, standing in the front window. She couldn't slow down, that would look suspicious. So, she kept driving and headed to switch her cars.

\#

Angela thanked her Lyft driver and got out of the car. She gave him a 4-star rating on her phone as she walked towards Barceloneta Miami. She always came here for happy hour. She loved the cheap drinks and always came home with a new flavor of the week! I will be babysitting Jelena this weekend, so I got to get something fresh for the next few days. She walked in the bar and noted people having dinner and singles at the bar. She spotted an empty seat at the end of the bar and headed over. As she walked a cute guy sitting at a table with what she assumed were his friends looked at her and winked. She gave him a flirtaious look. She knew she looked good in her little black dress that came down just an inch above her knees and red six-inch fuck 'em heels.

Mr. Office man, that's what she named him because he had on a suit with the tie askew and the top two buttons undone, downed the rest of his drink and leaned to his friend and whispered something as she took her bar stool. He looked as if he would get up. Angela pretended to check her phone and then glanced at the door. Mr. Office man deflated back into his chair. He had black hair short on the sides but longer in the front. You couldn't see his muscles through the suit, but you knew they were there. How much the suit fit it was an excellent tailor or a good body.

The bartender came over, a tall skinny kid with just a little muscle on him

"What can I get ya?"

"Can I have a sangria please?"

"Coming right at 'cha" he said and walked back to prepare her drink. She didn't want company right away. She wanted to have at least her first glass of wine and scout first. The bartender brought her drink, and she put a $10 bill in his hand. She spun in the bar stool to case the rest of the place when she saw Cassidy Firestone sitting at a table, getting close to someone's ear.

She choked on her wine and spun around. She excused herself

ensuite to finish her routine.

Angela emerged from her bathroom in just enough time to take the food out of the oven. She placed it on the island to cool, and her phone buzzed.

Cassidy: Hey, you alone?

Angela smiled and sat on her couch with her phone. She took a selfie and wrote the caption 'I guess you will never know' on it.

Cassidy: OMG what happened to your face, are you all right?
Angela: ha, hilarious.

Angela sucked her teeth and tossed the phone on the couch and made her way back to the kitchen. What an ass, she thought. Angela put the pot pie in a bowl, grabbed a fork and mixed the crust and filling together. Angela walked over to the living room and turned back around to check if she turned the oven off. She didn't she thought so she put her food down on the cushion and went back to turn the oven off. On her way yet again back to the living room she grabbed her lap table. She bought it at Target and then cut a few inches off the legs, to make it fit her sitting on the couch. She then painted it a dark brown with orange around the border to match her living room.

Angela turned the TV on and turned it to HGTV. She dug into her food and stared at her phone. I will not check it, she thought to herself. She turned her attention back to the television. Out of the corner of her eye she saw a blue dot flash on her phone. Maybe it's a message from Jelena or mi Hermana, she thought. Angela pushed the lap table out a bit and sat back on the couch. She stared at her phone and signed and picked it up.

Cassidy: Aww I didn't mean to hurt your feeling baby
Angela: I am a big girl my feelings don't get hurt
Cassidy: Prefer naked Angela, anyway

Angela: I don't have time for you, I am busy.

Cassidy: Okay, I'll see you tomorrow. Here is a distraction.

And with that, he sent her a selfie of his own. It was a body shot, stopping just above all the important parts. Angela stared at the picture with her mouth wide open. Yeah, I will be distracted all right, she thought as he tossed her phone to the side. Every commercial, boring part of the show or any other time her mind drifted. She picked up her phone and scrutinized the picture. "Not one damn imperfection" she said out loud. Angela watched TV for a while longer and then turned it off. She cleaned up her space and went into the bedroom. Her plan was to get a little further in her book. She ended up on her bed with her vibrator and a phone turned on to Cassidy's picture.

"This is what I came to see" a deep voice said scaring Angela.

She jumped up from the bed, reaching under her pillow to grab for a weapon. By the time her feet hit the floor, she had her weapon pointed at the intruder. There she stood naked from the waist down, with a baby blue ratty tank top on. Moisture dripping down her leg with her vibrator on the bed. Holding her Glock 43.

Cassidy erupted in laughter. The bent over holding your stomach and wiping tears kind of laughter. Angela dropped the gun on the bed and reached to turn the vibrator off. "How the hell did you get in here?" she said, enraged and embarrassed; which made her even madder. Cassidy tried to speak, but the laughter overtook him. Angela stomped into the bathroom and grabbed her robe. When she entered the bedroom again, it looked like Cassidy had regained his composure, until he saw her. Then he erupted in laughter again.

"Get the hell out!" Angela yelled. "I am pressing charges, you broke into my house."

"Is it breaking in when one, the spare key is under the plant next to the door." She stared at him with her mouth agape. "Yes dear, I knocked and there was no answer. I see the mat and the pot and thought you wouldn't be stupid enough to leave a key there, but I was wrong," he said grinning. "When I went to try the key in the lock the door opened," he gestured wide with his hands to emphasize his surprise. "I called your name when I opened the door and you didn't respond. Now we know why," he said with a wink.

Angela glared at him "Give me my key and get the hell out, now!" she said, holding her hand out palm up. Cassidy tossed the key through the air and it landed on Angela's bed.

"Come on" he said "we were getting to the pleasurable part. Here I have something better" he said as he began lifting his shirt. This made her cheeks burn with embarrassment, she was humiliated and her default emotion for humiliation was anger. Her cheeks burned even redder, but this time she was pissed. "Lárgate de mi casa antes de que te rompa el cuello-" <get out of my house before I break your neck>

She rambled on as she started walking towards him. Cassidy put his hands up in surrender motion "whoa no comprende, ingles ingles" he said. She was in arm's reach and punched with her right hand. He had enough time to sway out of the way when her left hand came charging in. Cassidy put both hands up in front of his face saying "okay, I get it I'm leaving" he turned and bee lined for the door.

Angela followed him the whole way and slammed the door as soon as he thought it. She put the spare key in the bowl by the door and went back into her bedroom. She grabbed her phone and called Jelena.

Jelena: Hello, Qué pasa, chica? <what's up girl>

Angela: Cass - er Firestone just caught me with my vibrator AND A PICTURE OF HIM!

Jelena: Hold on, I have multiple questions: When did we go from Firestone to Cassidy? Where did you get a picture of him? And how did he catch you?

Angela launched into the entire story on what happened with Jelena listening on the other end. Once she was finished, she let Jelena respond. When she was quiet Angela squealed "Jelena" into the phone. Jelena took a deep breath and replied, "send me the pic." Angela chuckled and sent over the picture real quick. Angela knew when Jelena had received it because she gasped and said "mi Dios, girl why did you send him away?" Angela chuckled and exhaled, she relaxed.

"Gracias chica" she said "te quiero."

"That's what I am here for," Jelena said with a smile in her voice.

Sandra and Smith welcome to the family

Sandra woke up Thursday morning feeling refreshed. She got all the things together in her new, temporary home. Jake was in the bed next to her still sleeping. She looked at him and smiled. She loved the fake lives she made for herself. This was bliss and she would live in this blissfulness as long as she could. Sandra slid out of bed and headed to the shower. Today is the BBQ, she thought. Her one and only chance in getting into the auction. She wanted to make a wonderful impression and she would. When she was finished with her shower, she turned off the water and stepped out of the glass door. She jumped, startled seeing Jake sitting on the toilet. Jake chuckled a little and said, "Good morning to you too." Sandra smiled and went over to the mirror over the sink.

"Today we have the BBQ, it starts in an hour."

"Have they have invited us to this BBQ?" he asked looking at her.

"It is a block party, we live on the block there for they invite us" she said looking at him through the mirror mounted on the wall. Sandra wrinkled up her nose

"You smell like ass," she said, plugging her nose.

Jake chuckled, "well get out." Sandra did just that and left the bathroom. As soon as she finished dressing, she heard the doorbell. She opened the door and saw her father standing there. "Daddy" she squealed. He shuffled past her

"Don't have me standing out here in the open, let me in" he grumbled as he passed her and went straight for the kitchen. "What are you doing in Miami?" her father asked as he went to the refrigerator and grabbed a beer. She followed him into the kitchen.

"This is my home daddy, what do you mean?"

"The last time you were here I told you when you leave to stay gone" He turned towards her, leaning on the countertop next to the refrigerator.

"Daddy, I was gone for a long time-"

"What are you planning?" he cut her off and asked.

Sandra rolled her eyes and turned around to walk out of the room. "Sandra Highworth, you better answer me" he bellowed. Just then Jake walked into the kitchen. He walked over to Sandra's father and held his hand out

"Hello sir," he said. Before he had time to finish the introduction Sandra's father screamed "leave us" Sandra stepped in "Daddy don't be rude. He is a guest in my house-" Jake put his hands up in a surrender motion and backed away "it's fine Sandra, I'll head over to the BBQ. Meet me over there when you wrap up here. Sandra blanched

"I forgot about the party" she turned to her father

"Daddy, I have to go. I'll call you later?" He walked up to her and grabbed her arm

"You are not going anywhere"

"Whoa" Jake stepped it "Too far buddy"

He turned and scowled at Jake "who the hell are you to tell

me anything" pointing a finger in his face.

He yanked Sandra's arm and jerked her back and forth. Jake grabbed his arm "That is enough, let go of her"

"Whatever she hired you for this is not in your job description, go wherever you need to go" he stared at Jake daring him to say something else. Sandra looked at Jake teary eyed

"You go to the party and mingle. I will be over there soon." Jake looked at her with disbelief. Sandra stared at him, pleading with her eyes for him to just drop it and go. Jake's eyes widened a fraction, and he turned and left the house.

Sandra's father, still holding on to her arm, walked her over to the dining room and sat her in a chair. When he let go of her arm, she had a hand print that wrapped around her arm. She stared up at him, still crying, and told her father her entire plan. He looked down at her with disgust in his eyes.

"Take the money and leave Miami, never come back." he said, and he walked out of the house. Sandra sat there and sobbed.

Jake was down the street at the party and had a beer in one hand and a burger in the other. He was standing with a group of husbands who were all making fun of what their kids had done. He excused himself and walked over to an older lady sitting by herself.

"Not too much of a mingling?" he said, smiling down at her. She smiled up at him

"Just enjoying the scenery. I've lived in this neighborhood all my life, I'm sad to know it is ending." Jake choked on his beer, "You're Danielle Price?"

She chuckled "Yes young man and you are?" she said looking up at him "I am uh J - er Smith, Smith Stoneybrooke."

Danielle's eyebrows rose "a Stoneybrooke, eh?" Danielle

turned in her chair so she faced Jake a little more.

"We just moved into the neighborhood, my wife and I. Jane Stoneybrooke." He said, watching her facial expressions.

"A man who took his wife's name." she looked at him.

Jake chucked, "You don't know my wife ma'am, there was no way I was getting her to change her name. Not because the name is famous, though. because 'who do I think I am dealing with a 1920 woman'" he mocked Sandra's voice. Danielle laughed.

"That is a terrible impression of me darling" he heard Sandra say. Jake cursed himself because he had forgotten his French accent. He turned towards Sandra "There you are dear" he said to her as he turned towards her and kissed her on the cheek.

"This is Danielle Price, Danielle this is my wife Jane." Sandra squinted her eyes at him and bent down to kiss Danielle twice, once on each cheek.

"Danielle, how are you darling?" Sandra asked. Sandra took a step back and slid into Jake's embrace. He stood with his arm around her shoulders.

"I am enjoying making these memories" she responded and turned her attention back to her lawn.

Groups of people gathered, kids running around with three different grills out with the smell of BBQ in the air. There were games of lawn bowling, corn husk and jumbo Jenga. There were kids with hula hoops, jump ropes, and sidewalk chalk. Everyone looked glad, like a postcard or a television commercial. For a moment Sandra let herself get lost in her surroundings. She got lost in the block party in a suburban neighborhood with a husband. Sandra snuggled into Jake's arm and took his beer to take a drink.

Danielle asked them, "what made you guys move into the

neighborhood?"

"We just moved from France," Sandra replied. Danielle's eyes widened, and she put her hand over her chest "my word" she said a thick southern accent coming through. She then turned to look at them

"What brought ya'll all the way from France?" Sandra gazed up at Jake, expecting him to answer the question. Jake panicked. He didn't know what to say.

"She goes and I follow," he said. Seemed like a safe enough answer, he thought to himself. Sandra giggled and put a hand on his chest.

"My mother and I switched continents," she told Danielle. Just then Danielle got up from her chair. Jake rushed to go help but got waved off.

"Let a dying woman have her sense of independence," she said as she walked over to a table with food and coolers. She got two plastic cups and poured a pink liquid into them. She walked back over to Jake and Sandra and handed Sandra the second cup.

"Beer is much too harsh for a lady dear" she said as she sat back in her chair. Sandra took the cup and handed Jake back his beer.

"Thank you, ma'am," she said. They sat there in a comfortable silence. Watching the party happen around them. Jake left and came back with a couple chairs. They sat down, a comfortable distance from Danielle, and Sandra reminisced on what could have been.

#

If her father wasn't controlling and abusive, if her mother hadn't abandoned her when she was a little girl, if stealing wasn't the only way to get the things the other high school girls had, if she didn't need aliases, if she could be in one place for more than a few years, if she meet someone and be honest with them, if her father could stand to be in the same city has her, only if she thought to herself. Sandra looked out across all the people and noticed everyone was staying away from Danielle.

"Danielle," she started "if we are disturbing you, we can move."

Danielle waved her hands "nonsense" she said. Sandra, and Jake too, were expecting her to say something else, but she didn't. The comfortable silence continued, and the party went on. The three of them sat there like that for a while.

"What do you two do?" Danielle said out of the blue.

Jake looks at Sandra and then at Danielle "I am a - uh - antiques dealer" he said.

"And Jane does a lot of charity work."

Sandra jumped in "real estate looks interesting to me, I am thinking of getting into that." Danielle didn't respond to them. Jake felt this need to fill the silence, a need he didn't feel until now. It's kind of weird to ask for a conversation starter and then stop talking, he thought.

"I go from place to place authenticating items people bring to me," he began "then I sell them to, well, a lot of unique places."

Danielle sipped her drink and closed her eyes. While her eyes were shut she took several deep breaths "what area do you specialize in?" she asked and then turned her head towards Jake to gage his reaction. Jake looked at her stunned but recovered.

"Furniture and books" he responded.

"And you're just living off mommy's money dear?"

"No ma'am, I have many interests I pursue" Sandra said, kind of offended.

"Interests and a job is not the same thing is it?" Danielle was still looking at the two of them very, scrutinizing everything.

"You are correct ma'am" Sandra said tight-lipped "I have never had an actual job. It has blessed me to pursue my interests without fear of financial insecurity,"

"And does putting on a French accent make you feel better, or is that to convince others of your importance?"

"Ma'am?" Sandra said looking at Danielle. Her eyes kept shifting back and forth between Jake and Danielle. Jake had a 'don't ask me' look on his face.

"You heard me dear" Danielle's eyes seem to get smaller by the second, her squint getting more and more intense.

"I was born here ma'am, in the south. My mother moved us to France when I was little. Growing up I caught on pretty quick that southern accents were not accepted in the circles I was trying to run in, I had to adapt."

"Hmm" Danielle said "so it's to convince others of your importance" Danielle sat there for a minute digesting what she had heard. Sandra and Jake sat there in silence watching the older lady.

"Well, you don't have to convince me of your importance so drop that accent while you're talking to me. Ya hear?"

Jake and Sandra exhaled in sync "yes ma'am" Sandra said letting her southern drawl come through.

"I'm old dear, but I am not dumb" Danielle said finishing her drink. She handed the empty cup to Jake "take care of this for me son" she asked him. Jake got up and ventured around looking for a trash can. Danielle turned in her chair and looked at Sandra.

"What is it I can do for you?"

"We are just here to enjoy our new neighborhood."

"My parties are always open to everyone in the neighborhood. I turn no one down. However, young lady, as you can see everyone else is off enjoying the party. You and your Husband Smith are sitting here with me. That leads me to believe you need something for me."

Sandra panicked damn this lady she thought to herself. Sandra decided the truth was the best way to get herself out of this scrutiny. "Ma'am," she began, "this is a reality that I've only dreamed of. Seeing all of this" Sandra gestured across the lawn "so I guess mingling will take away from me needing to soak it in."

Sandra looked up at the sky and blinked a few times to clear the tears from her eyes. Danielle looked at her and said "now dear, that is the most honest thing you have said to me yet." Danielle shifted in her chair again so she could see the yard and her neighbors. Sandra sat back into her chair and relaxed. Her phone buzzed, and she reached into her pocket to check it.

Jake: Am I all clear to come back.
Sandra: Yea, she knew that we were lying!
Jake: Damn, she's good. What now?
Sandra: ¯_(ツ)_/¯

Jake walked back over and bent over closer to Sandra's ear "Hey I am going over with that group of guys, okay?"

"Yes, you go have fun" Sandra said smiling up at him. Sandra and Danielle watched Jake walk away. "What's his actual name anyway?" Danielle said. That surprised Sandra, causing her to look at Danielle with widened eyes.

"Oh, please" Danielle said while waving her hand in a dismissive gesture.

"Jake," Sandra whispered.

"Jake" Danielle said his name, letting it roll around on her tongue. "Jake and who?" Danielle asked.

Sandra sat back in her chair and stared at Jake over with the group of guys having fun. I am about to fuck up everything she thought to herself. "Jake and Sandra" she said just above a whisper "We are Jake and Sandra."

"Dear," Danielle said after a few moments of silence, "I am having an auction of my estate soon. I am sure you and your Antiques Dealer would love to attend. I'll put you on the list."

"Oh no," Sandra said, rethinking her plan now that Danielle knew her actual name, "We couldn't impose."

Danielle waved her hand "nonsense" she said "September 8th, I'll have someone drop off an invitation for you." Danielle got up from her seat and sauntered to a table and picked up a paper plate. Sandra watched her walk over to one grill and started talking to a tall gentleman.

Jake walked over to her and sat in the chair "I think it's time to go home" he said.

"Why would you say that?" Sandra replied.

Jake put his hand on her shoulder and turned her towards him "because you're crying Sandra - er Jane."

"Sandra is fine" she said, "Danielle calls me Sandra"

Jake looked at her in disbelief, "and what does she call me?" he asked.

"Jake, we're Sandra and Jake."

Torture, poke and prod

Jelena was still suspended in the air. How long has it been, I'm so sore, it feels like days? I don't think my toes can stand anymore. I have to relax; I have to get off my toes. Jelena is turned, so that she is looking at the 5 ladies in the eyes. All these lives lost, they were mothers and daughters. She sobs trying to work her aching toes to turn herself so she is not staring at the horror in the face. She freezes as she hears footsteps, then the door creaks open and she hears the footsteps down the stairs. They are slow and deliberate done to extract the most fear out of her. She knew this and still could not stop the pure terror coursing through her bones.

"Hello Jelena, have you had time to think about your behavior." I walk around her inspecting as much as I can. I haven't turned on the light. The dark is a necessity. She is still standing on her toes but they are a mixture of black, blue and purple. Looks like they will fall off. The poor thing is lasting longer than my other ones.

"Even more fun for me." I walked over to my table and clanked all my tools to ensure they made a noise and then peeked and watched her squirm. I picked up my favorite tool and walked over to her, sliding my feet along the way. She is sucking in deep breaths trying to stop herself from crying.

"Aww, your going to be stong and not cry," I say as I scrape the pointed hook along her skin, digging just enough to make a cut. Then I insert the hook and separate the skin from the muscle underneath. She cringes and sends out a piercing scream and then stops when she realizes she can't do it without losing the balance on her toes. This makes me laugh out loud and hard.

He's laughing, why is this so funny to him. I am trying to be brave and not give him anything to feed off of but he likes this just as much as when I cry and scream. It feels like he is trying to separate my skin from my body. I cannot move or scream without losing the balance on my toes. My toes hurt so much I should just end my misery. There is no way for me to survive this, I should just give up. I let my feet relax and feel the shooting pain coming up from my toes all the way through to my fingertips. My airways constrict but I am not choking. This must be a sign, a sign from God, that it's my time. As soon as I close my eyes welcoming what's next. I heard the loud crank and I began dropping to the floor.

My eyes pop open and, in my mind, I say "what's happening" but the words don't turn into the sound to come out. The ground is freezing and shoots needles through my body. But I collapse and savor the feeling of being on solid ground and not suspended into the air. My chain gets yanked. I jerked to the side startled by the sudden movement and terrified I forgot he was in the room.

"You thought we were done?" he asked me. His voice was raspy, like he was trying to make it sound that way but it was not normal.

TORTURE, POKE AND PROD

"Come here Jelena," he says as he yanks my hair so hard the chunk that was in his hand was no longer attached to head. I let out a loud yelp and grabbed for the now bald spot on my head. He took whichever tool he had and sliced the backside of my palm and I shrieked. I brought my hand, bleeding, to my shirt, or what was left of my shirt.

"Put pressure and that would stop the bleeding." I thought to myself. He grabbed my arm and tied something around it and the same to the other one. Now my hands were sprawled out to either side of me like I was reaching outwards.

"Time to have fun" He says. He then cranks my neck lever back up and ties each ankle to something I can't quite see. Next thing I know I sprawled in the air spread eagle.

I go back towards my table and grab another tool. I walk to her and put the long blade in her face so even in the dark light she can see what it is and then I watch the pure terror as recognition splashes across her face. I chuckle and then poke and prod my way around until I am satisfied. An hour later I go back up the stairs to make a snack, all that work has left me famished. I walked into the kitchen and heard my phone ring from another room. I went in search of it and picked it up just in time.

Hello

Is it done?

Almost

Hurry, stop playing around and finish the job.

These things take time Sup-

Don't say my name! Just do what I'm paying you to do.

With that the caller hung up. 'Who does he think he is talking

to me like that? I will take just as much time as I please. This work takes patience and mastery of skills, which I have both'. I go back into the kitchen to finish my snack and realize I haven't brought the sweet Jelena any water or food in a few days. I grab a cup of water and a sleeve of saltine crackers and head back downstairs. I forgot I suspended her in the air. I release her arms and neck chains and levers so she is hanging upside down and I place the water and crackers at her head just in reach for her to grab them, but have to struggle to do so. Satisfied I turn and head back upstairs. When I reach the top of the stairs, I turn back and look at her and see her fingertips trying to grasp the crackers, I grin and close the door.

Sorry, not sorry, move on

Later Thursday night Jelena was in the mirror taking off her makeup when Dan walked into the bedroom.

"Lo Siento" he said as he stared at her through her reflection in the mirror. She paused to return his gaze and then returned to what she was doing. After she finished her routine, she collected the book she was reading from her nightstand and headed towards the door. She stopped in the doorway and said without looking at him.

"Too little too late, let's move on" and then walked out of the bedroom. She went downstairs to the kitchen and poured a glass of wine. She went into the den, sat, and began reading her book. Dan stood upstairs dumbfounded.

What does she mean "let's move on," he thought? Dan stood there for a minute gathering his thoughts and then went to get some work done. Going down to the office and tried to focus on the task at hand but he couldn't, he kept thinking about Jelena and what she meant by "move on". He got up from his desk and got dinner started. Dan headed into the kitchen and rummaged through the cabinets and refrigerator to see what there was to eat. He decided on fish and potatoes. He put on his pod-cast and began cooking. Before he knew it, the food was in the oven and about 35 minutes had passed. He walked through the house and came upon Jelena in the den.

"Hey hon, food on. It will be about 30 minutes" he said. She glanced up from her book and gave him a blank stare. He looked at her and tilted his head to the side.

"Everything okay?"

She shook out of her stupor, "sorry this book is just intense. So I don't read thrillers or suspense because I analyze everything. But I can't seem to put them down."

Dan went into the room and sat in the chair opposite his wife "what's happened so far." Jelena put her bookmark in the book and closed it. She switched her position, so she was facing him, and went into the elaborate plot of her psychological thriller. After what seemed like 10 or 15 minutes of her talking. Dan put his hand on his chin in deep thought. Jelena sighed

"You think I'm being stupid." He looked at her

"No, I'm thinking, trying to get a grasp on both sides."

She sat up a little straighter "Okay so tell me what you think."

They then launched into a conversation about her book and he did an outstanding job playing devil's advocate, getting her to see the sides of all the characters in the book. The bell interrupted them on the oven. Dan got up and went into the kitchen while Jelena went to set the table. In a few minutes they came together at the table and got back into the conversation about the book. They finished their dinner and began picking up the table.

"So how did work go today?" she asked.

He explained the newest job he was working on and the difficulties he has been encountering. They cleaned off the table and then went into the den and sat on the couch. Jelena sat with both her legs curled underneath her sitting sideways while Dan was sitting with one leg crossed over the other. He was in the arm's nook so he could turn to see Jelena.

"It's just difficult" he continued "I am trying to be creative and deliver something new but the client seems to want the same style as everyone else."

Jelena pondered that for a moment and said, "You think of your work as your art correct?"

"Yes" he replied.

"Okay then, maybe it is time you expand your business." She held up her hands in stop motion, "hear me out. You can still take on clients and do their building the way they are paying you to do them. That's what it is, you getting paid to deliver their vision, not your vision." She paused and tilted her head to the side, looking at him, then she continued. "Take on a business partner and start a business building your own buildings in your own vision and just have your partner fill you in with some business and you would give them a percentage of the business." She stared at him, watching his eyes swivel in his head as he thought it over.

He said, "What about your wife?" Her face scrunched up, and she looked at him with a puzzled look.

"What about your wife what?"

He replied, "If you had to open a business, what would it be?"

She sat back a bit and thought about that. "Well" She began "Off the top of my head I think clothes and food smell great. So, I would do one of those" she stared at him trying to gage his response.

He said, "I like your idea of me building my own buildings. But I figure why I need a business partner when I could just go into business with my wife-"

"Because your wife doesn't know the first thing about business" she interrupted. They finished talking and throwing ideas back and forth. Around 11:00 pm they went upstairs. Jelena hopped in the shower while Dan took the clothes from the upstairs dryer and folded them. After about 45 minutes of night routine, they were in bed reading.

"This was a pleasant night," Dan said.

"Just a normal one" Jelena replied. She put her book down, reached over to turn off her light and then rolled over.

The next morning Jelena awoken to the alarm on her phone going off. She rolled over in bed, stretching out and realized Dan was already up. Talk about normal, she thought to herself. Dan was always,, up before her, and she never heard his alarm. She rolled back to reach for her phone and shut the song off that played in place of the traditional beep beep beep of normal alarms. Jelena sat up in bed and scrolled. She scrolled down her Google news and saw another woman had been missing in the Great Palm Area suburb.

"Damn" she said "that is like 5 in the past few months" Jelena went to her contacts and clicked on Monica Cornwell who worked the kidnapping cases, she answered on the third ring

Monica: This is Cornwall

Jelena: Hey, this is Cohert. How are you?

Monica: Good girl! How has it been?

Jelena: Girl, working this fresh case. I need something unrelated to what I am working on.

Monica: What's up?

Jelena: Is anything happening with all the girls I see in the news?

Monica: oh, the missing girl. No girl, we don't have any evidence to say there might have been foul play. Until then, it ties our hands.

Jelena: If something comes up, you'll let me know?

Jelena hung up the phone, and types in the Google search bar missing woman Miami suburbs. She spent the next few minutes going through articles.

"Jelena" Dan Called "come eat, I've got 10 minutes before I have to head out."

Jelena got out of bed and walked towards the bathroom door. She got her robe she had hanging on the door and headed downstairs.

"Hey babe" she said walking into the kitchen. Jelena made a beeline for the island and sat at a bar stool. Dan came and put two plates on the countertop. Jelena grabbed her fork and dug in.

"You know how I feel about Omelets and Hash," she said as she shoveled food into her mouth. "How did you sleep?" she asked.

"Well, how about you?" Dan said as he sat down and ate.

"Yeah, I slept well. Hey, did you know there is another missing girl over in Great Palms?"

"No I didn't know that," he said kind of.

Jelena looked at him, "that is like 10 miles from here Dan. That is the 5th girl to go missing in the last couple months. That doesn't bother you?"

Dan continued eating as if not appearing by the information "I choose to not pay attention to the evil things in the world."

"That is naïve" Jelena said rolling her eyes "Naive you are if you believe life favors those who aren't naïve" she quoted Piet Hein and continued eating.

Dan looked at her and squinted his eyes. "Why should I focus on that negativity?" he asked her.

"Dan there has been five missing women in the suburbs of Miami within the last few months. All women in their late 30s out running or walking. That isn't alarming to you?"

"Jelena" Dan said taking a breath, "I choose not to care, you shouldn't either"

Jelena sucked her teeth and scowled at him "even if I wasn't in the FBI I am still a decent person. If you will excuse me I have to get ready for work. Have a wonderful day" she said and pushed her stool back leaving her unfinished food on the island and went upstairs. Dan sat there with his mouth agape looking in the direction Jelena just went. His phone beeped, and he shook his head and pulled it out of his inside jacket pocket. "Time to go," he said and put his dishes in the sink and rushed out of the door.

Upstairs, Jelena grabbed her phone and called Angela. She put the phone on speaker.

Angela: Hey girl, what's up? I am on my way to meet Firestone now.

Jelena: Girl, did you see the article on the 5 missing girls?

Angela: Yes!! Girl, aww man that is right next to you isn't it?

Jelena: I know, Monica said, there isn't a case yet because there is no evidence of foul play. She's coming with us Saturday.

Angela: Si Si, that's fine I love Monica. They won't mess with you though, you're a badass chick. But Jelena, I am at HQ I'll hit you up later, okay?

Jelena: No problem. I have things to do today I should get started on.

The ladies hung up with each other. Jelena hopped in the shower. After she had gotten dressed, she went through the house searching for her briefcase. She wasn't even sure she brought it home with her. After spending a few minutes searching, she gave up and got her keys to go switch cars. Finding her briefcase in the black SUV. She was in the car listening to Sirius xm fly, 90s and 2000, r&b and hip hop and headed to the field office. She needs to do some legwork for those warrants.

Cohert got to her office and noticed her door was ajar. She stopped and looked around. Hmm, she thought I always check to make sure my door clicks. Cohert got into her office and put her stuff down. When she sat in her chair, she picked up the phone and called the maintenance number. "Hey Mike" she said into the phone "I was just checking to see if anyone has asked to be let into my office. Yup, uhuhh. Great thanks Mike." Cohert hang up the phone and marched to Romanary's office. She didn't bother knocking, she opened the door and Romanary, Boss and two other gentlemen she didn't recognize was in the room. Cohert walked right up to Romanary and got into his face.

"I hope you have enjoyed your promotion and your new office. It's over now, and you touch my office door one more time" she squinted and got right up in his face "and I'll have your entire job." She turned on her heels, acknowledging no one in the room. Cohert went straight back to her office and dialed a four digit extension on her phone.

"Hello this is Deputy Director Dominguez's office, how many I help you?"

"Hello Renee, this is -"

"Jelena dear" the lady on the other line squealed into the phone.

"Hola cariño" Cohert said smiling. She loved Renee, had ever since she was a child. Renee has been there for her. "I need to speak to papí" Cohert explained.

"No hay problema" Renee said and then said "Senor Dominguez, a phone call from Senior Special Agent Dominguez" she yelled sounding muffled, like her hand was over the receiver. Cohert waited a few moments and then heard a deep vibrate voice on the phone "Hija! How are you?" her father asked.

"Papí, did you tell René I'm married? My name is Cohert"

Her father gave a deep belly laugh, "now hija, something's we just have to let go, and this is one of those things. How has my girl been?"

"I am on the Sandra Highworth case. I think we are getting along pretty well."

"Ah yes, I've heard of the hardships that come along with that. It's good that you and your team are making headway. What can I do for you?"

"I need someone demoted. Romanary, he is incompetent and asked maintenance to open my office to snoop through my materials. He is not supposed to be -"

"Jelena, I hear you. I will send the paperwork through. You do not ask for work favors so I know this must be big. Consider it done by the end of the day."

"Gracias papí,"

"I know we have some hardships. I am still your father and I still have your back."

Jelena hung up the phone and sat at her desk quiet for a minute. She shut her eyes and took some deep breaths. Once she had herself together she turned on her computer and checked her email. She was looking for emails about whether she could exhume those bodies. She was going through the list when her door slammed open.

"You got me demoted!" Romanary screamed across the room. Cohert looked up at him and then turned her attention back to her computer. Romanary stormed across the room and pulled the chair she was sitting in around. Cohert jumped up and got into a wide stance, ready for anything. Romanary had her but a few inches and at least 75 pounds, but she wasn't backing down.

"I advise you to back up out of my face," Cohert said very.

"Who did you have to get on your knees for to make that happen?"

Cohert smirked at him, and that seemed to make him enraged. Assistant Special Agent in Charge Monroe entered the room.

"Agent Romanary I need you to back up out of her face," he said with a deep authoritative voice. Romanary turned around and faced Monroe.

"Sir, I am sure you know that I just got my title revoked. This happened right after Cohert came into my office and threatened me."

"Agent Romanary I understand that you manipulated your way into Agent Cohert's office to get into information that classified to you."

Romanary recoiled and stifles back a groan. "Sir, I am a Senior Agent, the information I was seeking was information I have clearance for," Romanary said, still standing at attention.

"Agent, if you had clearance you wouldn't need to go sneaking around. I made no mistake picking who I wanted to lead this task force and who I wanted to have knowledge of the day-to-day mechanics. Now this demotion has come in over my head, you or I have no choice. However, if this had been brought to my attention," Monroe looked at Cohert "you would have received discipline."

"Romanary's eyes bulged in his head "why does everyone stick up for this bitch" he spit with much venom as he turned his head to the side to stare at Cohert through his peripheral, still giving her his back.

"Romanary, you need to leave my office. Now." Cohert said in a calm voice, raising her voice an octave when she said the word now.

"I am not going anywhere you immigrant bitch" Romanary said, still only giving her his back.

"Parker Romanary," Monroe barked, "that is no way to talk to your superior. You are out of line. We do not accept racial or gender discrimination. Agent Cohert will file a formal complaint with HR to add to your many other complaints. You make the FBI look bad for Peter, which puts you on thin ice. Now that I know that there is an ongoing issue you need to clean yourself up, or the Deputy Director won't get the chance to fire you."

Monroe looked at Romanary's face as it beat red. Romanary asked Monroe "am I excused sir" he bit out under tight lips.

"Yes," Monroe said.

In the hall, Romanary slammed the door shut and stalked to his office. "The fucking Deputy Director" he mumbled under this breath. He got to his office, and Boss was standing at his door. Romanary spoke up before Boss had the chance "Boss if you don't mind I need a minute to compose myself."

"You don't have a minute Romanary, you have 10 minutes to clear out this office and bring your things to cubicle 0012"

"0012' Romanary shouted "the 00 cubicles are on the first floor."

"We have to rearrange a few things" the Boss scolded, "no one expected to need to move people around. Now I need to promote a Senior Agent because the one I had is incompetent" boss said, voice growing louder and louder as he finished the sentence.

Romanary opened his mouth to say something but got cut off by Boss. "There is a paper trail of you being racist and sexist from multiple different women. There is a paper trail of your incompetence and instead of keeping your head down, your mouth shut and just do your DAMN job you break into the office of the DEPUTY DIRECTOR's DAUGHTER and try to access CLASSIFIED files. Get your shit and move." Boss finished his rant, huffing, out of breath. He looked at Romanary, daring him to reply at all, walked past him going back to his office. A few seconds later a door slammed shut.

Romanary went into the office and picked up two picture frames off his desk. He then smashed his computer monitor off the desk and all the surrounding papers on to the floor. He kicked the piled up boxes of files, and they scattered all over the floor. He threw the desk chair across the room and then walked out.

Monroe stood in front of Cohert "you went to dad?" Monroe said looking hurt.

"He is a bastard and a pig and since he is part of your little boy's club, he gets away with it. The man broke into my office. I am fine with people not knowing my unfortunate family lineage. You are the one who told him that, not me. What I won't do is sit around and be disrespected by you, Jackson, Romanary or anyone else." Cohert stared at her with passion in her eyes. Passion filled with rage and pain.

"I am your brother Jelena, you can lean on me"

"Maybe the child Jelena could lean on her brother and father. The Jelena victim Jelena who died and the survivor who emerged know she doesn't have you or your father in her corner." Cohert straightened her shoulders and took a step back "Now sir" she bit out "if you would please excuse me, I have exhumation orders and warrants to follow up on. I am working a time sensitive case"

Monroe looked at Cohert and said just above a whisper, "I'm sorry" and then turned and left his office. He was walking down the hall when Romanary stormed past him. He walked towards Romanary's office and saw they destroyed the room. Monroe rolled his eyes and pulled out his phone. He sent a text 'send maintenance to Romanary's office. Clean and change name tag'. Monroe slipped his phone back in his pocket and walked towards the elevator.

In her office, Cohert sits at her computer and closes her eyes. She put the middle and ring finger on each hand and rubbed her temples in a circular motion. She stays like that for a few minutes and then ran her hands down her cheeks and then back up and covers her face. Cohert has not spoken with her brother, the Assistant Special Agent in Charge Mr. Oliver Monroe, in months. All of their communications have been through email, text messages or a third party.

She knew he wasn't pissed because she went to their father. He was pissed because she went over his head. She hated the stupid boy's club. Women get treated in unspeakable ways in and out of the workplace and all men do is sit around, make excuses for each other and laugh about it. They knew how Romanary was. He harassed women. They knew he called her and Ang immigrants. It was okay, though; he is a part of the boy's club just like her brother and father.

Jelena was in an abusive relationship when she was 22. She was fresh out of college with her bachelor's degree in criminal psychology and trying to figure out what to do with herself. She met Alejandro Ramírez. Her papí had introduced him to her. He told them he had his bachelor's degree in criminal justice, but it was taking him an extra year to get a minor in social work. These were all lies. He was from Mexico and had traveled to the United States and had become a citizen which was also a lie. He lived on campus, he said, but was looking for an apartment to save on some costs, which was also a lie. Papí loved him. He put them on the fast track to marriage. Alexandro worked at a coffee shop, and all the employees, and regular customers, loved him. He was nice and smart. When they were dating for a few months he started staying at her house more and more. She thought nothing about it. She was falling hard for him. When Monroe came home from duty they became best friends.

Alexandro and Jelena were living together, in Jelena's house, after six months of dating and married within the first year. The entire family loved him, Jelena loved him. The wedding was a grand event, papí wouldn't expect anything less. That day, April 3rd, was the best day of her life. It was also the first day of the worst time in her life. The first time he hit it stunned her her. He slapped her across her face so hard she stumbled back a little. She never thought she would be that girl. Her dad and her brother were hefty men. They had thought she let no one disrespect her. She does not need a man to depend on.

When she told her brother he had slapped her, Oliver asked her "what did he do next?" He looked at her and apologized, and that's what she told her brother because that is what he did. Oliver told her it wasn't an enormous deal. He told her not to worry about it that time, and the next time, and the next time, and the next time. When the abuse got above five unique incidents, she stopped telling him. She told her father. Surly papí would not take this behavior happening to his little girl. Oliver told him first, but told him it was Jelena's fault. She started changing her behavior, trying not to make him mad. All that did was piss her off. She knew how a victim acted and talked. She knew she shouldn't be doing this, and that made her furious.

She started fighting back. That was her solution. 'I am not a victim if I fight back" she would say. Alexandra would go hang out with her Hermano and papí and come back and her and Alexandro would beat each other up. The day her father got promoted she went to the congratulation party, and she cried happy tears. Her makeup ran and showed all the bruising on her face. Her father played enraged in public and then told her to get a waterproof foundation in private. "Never let the public see your private life" he would tell her.

The day she went to the hospital is the day her life changed. She remembers it like it was yesterday. She was working with a non-profit organization counseling at-risk kids coming from detention or residential care transitioning back into a traditional community. She went to the foster home of one of her kids on her caseload to do an emergency session. She planned on 15 to 30 minutes tops but ended up being there for two hours. She came home late and as soon as she walked in the house, her house, he punched her in the face. She wasn't expecting the attack and lost consciousness. She was in the hospital for three weeks in a coma and another 6 months in physical therapy. The moment she woke up in the hospital, she vowed to change her life.

She turned to papí and Oliver for help when she was in physical therapy. Alejandro visited her every day like a wonderful husband, so neither papí nor Oliver agreed to go move her things out. She had decided to leave her husband, her house and her life and all her family would do was tell her to stick it out. "There is something that is making you two conflict" they would say "find out what that is and fix it." Papi would say, "I will not lose that marvellous man as a son-in-law, you need to fix it."

She hired movers, rented an apartment and joined the FBI academy the week she got finished with physical therapy. María Jelena Dominguez became Jelena M.D and changed to Jelena Cohert when Dan came into the picture.

"Fuck the boy's club" Cohert said out loud at her desk. Cohert shook her head as if to refocus herself and returned her attention to her emails. She had 15 more than she had the last time she sat down and she groaned. Cohert took a deep breath and got back to work.

Daddy, I need your help

Friday afternoon Slickey is sitting in her loft on her bean bag chair with her computer on her lap. "Okay girl, so I am trying to hack into their network just so I can get a look around, become familiar. But their securities are tight, fantastic" she bites her lip "I am not sure I can get in on my own."

Sandra was at her own computer sitting at the 4-seat table. She popped her head up from her screen and looked at Slickey. "Girl" She said with a hint of southern drawl "I can't afford to bring anyone else in. I can't have Jane in contact with more than one suspected hacker.

"No, I get it" Slickey said "and I am trying for real."

The two spent the morning and afternoon engrossed in their devices. They ate potato chips and drank naked juice along the way. Slickey got up from her spot and walked over to the table where Sandra was.

"Okay listen" She said as she plopped down beside her, "I got halfway in. I can see their past and present clients, and account details. I cannot seem to get into the Price account. It seems like all open accounts are under extra security."

Sandra looked at her "so what is our next move. This entire thing is built upon getting access to that account."

Slickey slumped back in the chair. "I will need to bring someone else in. I just can't do it by myself. I have been out of the game too long."

Sandra sat back in the chair and bit her lip. Right as she was about to respond, her computer started beeping. Both ladies looked at the screen and watched it turn black with green writing all on it and then it turned black.

Slickey's face turned white. "You've got to go," she said.

"Sandra stood "Wait, what happened, why?"

"Did you set me up" Slickey glared at Sandra.

"Set you up!" she bellowed "what the hell is going on?"

"They were tracking my hack, they just took possession of my computer and locked me out. I will jail." She said as she paced back and forth.

"Slickey" Sandra began "why would I set you up?"

Slickey began throwing Sandra's things at her "get your shit and go. The police are on the way and I have to figure out what to do."

Sandra stood there frozen in disbelief.

Slickey yelled, "Go!"

Gripping her things, Sandra headed towards the door. She tried to turn around and look at Slickey, but the door slammed in her face. "Great" she mumbled "what the fuck, and I supposed to do now."

Slickey was in a Grey concrete room. She sat in one metal chair while she stared at another one. She noticed there was no mirror. She knew she was in an interrogation room, however it didn't have a mirror. A lady walked in with a stern look on her face. A man followed in behind her looking more menacing, if that is even possible.

"Hello," the lady said, "Rachel Macwire, correct?"

Slickey slouched in her chair, "Yeah, that's me. I want a lawyer" she said with my arms folded across my chest.

She smiled at me, "you'll get one,. For right now you will answer my questions."

Slickey looked at her wide eyed and dumbfounded "I asked for my lawyer you can't talk to me anymore."

Cohert looked at Slickey "Listen, I was in the middle of important business when I get a call" Cohert lowered her voice to mimic a male's voice "Senior Special Agent Cohert, we have an important lead we need you to come in" her voice went back to normal.

"Then I get down here and it's a decade old hacker sitting in my interrogation room. So, Miss. Macwire you will get your lawyer after you answer my questions and before I offer you any immunity for the information, you may have."

Slickey's eyes got wide "nope this is against my rights I have nothing to say." Slickey jerked back in the chair and started staring around the room. Her eyes filled with tears what the hell Sandra got me into she thought.

Cohert signed heavenly, got up from the chair and left the room.

Boss followed behind her when his phone rang. He dug into his left pocket and looked at the screen; it was black. It put that phone back into his left pocket and reached for the other one in his right pocket. He answered on the 5th ring

Boss: hello

Caller: daddy, my friend got arrested and I need your help

Boss: what do you expect me to do about whatever misdemeanor you have gotten your friends into?

Caller: Daddy, we were shopping on the computer and wanted to see how many items of these pairs of boots they sold. So we might have hacked -

Boss: Your friend is a hacker. Oh, Sandy, *what the hell have you gotten*

Caller: Daddy can you -

Boss: I cannot help, goodbye

And with that, he jerked the phone into his pocket. Jelena stood round the corner listening to the one sided conversation. She couldn't hear what the person on the phone was saying. She heard the Boss say Sandy; she complemented this as she walked to her office. She didn't know any Sandy in her Boss's life. She knew he had two daughters. One was named Jennifer, she didn't know the second one's name though because he never talked about her. She pulled up the sticky note app on her computer and wrote who is Sandy. "Okay time for me to go home," she said aloud and walked out of her office. Hearing the click of the door before she walked off.

She passed Boss in the hallway "Cohert" he bellowed "Sir" she responded.

"What are your plans with the hacker?"

She looked at him and said, "the unies will put her in lock up and she will get her lawyer. I will deal with it on Monday." She looked at him, awaiting his reply. When he offered none she continued down the hall

"Do not walk away from me until I dismiss you," he hissed.

Cohert stopped and looked over her shoulder. She looked at him, flipped her hair and continued walking. The Supervisory Special Agent stood there with smoke coming from his ears. He stomped off to his office, slammed the door and pulled out his phone out of his left pocket. He dialed a number and held the phone to his ear.

Caller: Hello

Boss: Move up the timeline, I need her handled now

Caller: ahh Supervisory Special Agent. I am in the middle of a job for another client. I will be able to get to you in about a week and a half like we have discussed.

Boss: I am paying you a shit-load of money for me to be —

Caller: Listen Jackson

Boss: NEVER SAY MY NAME

Caller: You will have to wait in line and will keep my services based on our original agreement.

Then the caller hung up the phone. Boss sat there in disbelief and pure fury. He reached into his left pocket to get his work phone. His face blanched, going pale. He realized his left pocket was empty as he looked at the phone in his hand. "I used my work phone," he said aloud. "He used my name, he used my title" Boss held his head in his hands for a few moments. He then picked up his head, stood up and exited his office. He went down to the interrogation room.

Boss opened the door, "you a hacker?" he asked Slickey.

"I am not talking without my lawyer," she replied.

"I will release you on your own recognizance for a favor," he said.

Slickey sat up straight "I'm listening"

"I made a call on this phone, I need all records of this call erased off all platforms. Can you do it?"

Slickey looked at him in disbelief. Then she put her game face on. "You drop all charges and you have a deal"

Slickey saw a hint of defeat in his eyes and knew she went too far. Boss turned and left the room. "Shit!" Slickey yelled.

She sat there in the car and two uniformed officers came in. They

*handcuffed her and read her rights. "I have already read my rights,"
she said, irritated. The officer asked her again, "Do you understand
these rights ma'am?" Slickey puffed out a yes and was led out of
the building into a squad car.*

*At the jail, Slickey sat in a sizeable room with a lot of other people.
She had already been fingerprinted and had her picture taken. I
had put her into a holding cell in her own clothes. They had a TV
and a pay phone. The TV ran different bail bondsman numbers.*

*Slickey looked around the room and tore up. I told myself I would
never go to jail; she thought. The last time she got caught, the time
it took for her to quit illegal activity, she never made it to jail. She
cut a deal in the interrogation room. She now freelanced sort of
work for the government. That's what the government did when
they caught a good hacker, they put them to work for them.*

*When she was presented with this and she accepted, without
waiting for her lawyer to say something. She would do anything
to stay out of jail and I still would,* she thought. Why hadn't she
took that man's deal? Slickey looked at the phone and walked
over to it.

"I'll call Sandra," she said aloud "she got me into this mess
she can get me out."

Wolf in sheep's clothing

Jelena pulled into the second house to switch cars. She hated that she got interrupted and then the girl lawyered up, anyway. She got back into her car and pulled out of the garage, hitting the remote button on her way out. She pulled around the corner and noticed the house on the corner had new tenets. She made a mental note for her and her husband to go welcome them to the neighborhood. It made them seem friendly and helped her keep tabs on unfamiliar people coming in.

She pulled into her driveway and took the key out of the ignition. When she entered the house, she threw her keys on the side table and headed up to her room. She walked from the door to her bed, stepping out of her shoes along the way and collapsed on her bed. Not bothering to get under the covers or cuddle with her husband, she was asleep in minutes.

Jelena woke to an empty bed that she noticed once she stretched spread eagle on the bed. She lay there on the bed for a few moments, orienting herself, preparing to get up and get out of the bed. The boss called me saying they have caught the hacker that tried to gain access to Johnson & Jones systems, she thought. She lawyered up, won't be easy she thought as she rolled over to grab her phone. She sent her team a quick text

Cohert: got a suspect in custody. Rachel Macwire got caught by Johnson & Jones hacking into their systems. Clearweather and Bell get with the tech guys and get us a lead.

Belle: got it, boss

Clearweather: Today?

Rodriguez, Firestone, Michaels: Got it

Cohert: enjoy your weekend, we will start fresh on Monday

Jonathan: got it, boss

The next morning, Jelena groaned and rolled out of bed. She stripped out of her clothes she wore to the office earlier, put on her Robe and slipped into her slippers. Jelena padded down the stairs looking for Dan. He was in the kitchen. She knew this because she heard his podcast playing. She walked over and entered the kitchen "always cooking" she said as she walked over to the stove peeking into the pots.

Dan swatted her away "women, what would you do without me cooking. Oh, I know you would die"

Jelena sat on the stool on the opposite side of the island.

Dan put down the spoon and walked over to Jelena "I have to use the bathroom, don't let it burn" he said as he kissed her on the forehead.

As he left the room Jelena went to the stove to inspect the pots. What a mess, she thought as she started taking vegetable peels and other food things off the counter putting it into the garbage disposal. She cleaned the island and dumped the stuff in the trash. Noticing the trash was full, she reached in trying to grab the bag to take it for the dumpster. The bag caught, and the can tipped over out of the cabinet. She cursed and picked up the trash can, set it aside. When she looked in the cabinet, she saw a book. She paused and looked at it.

"Hey, are you in there letting my food burn" Dan said as he walked back into the kitchen. He halted as he saw the scene in front of him. His wife with a garbage bag in her hands, the cabinet open and staring into the cabinet. Oblivious to him entering the room, she set the trash bag down and reached inside and grabbed his journal out. Think fast Cohert, Dan thought. "How the he- babe you found my journal. I've been looking for this all week" He walked over to her and reached for the journal.

"What is it doing under the trash can? Why hide it from me?" He did a nervous laugh

"Honey, honestly, I lost it. I didn't put it there on purpose."

She stared at him in disbelief. Jelena walked over to him and handed him the journal. "This would've been just as safe on the dresser or nightstand then it was under the trash can" she walked past him and headed to the inside garage door. She stepped into the garage and walked over to the trash can. As she put the bag in the can, she thought to herself he hid it from me. She looked down at herself and wish she had on clothes so she could go on a run.

After going back into the house and upstairs to put on workout gear, Jelena was out of the house. Her feet hit the pavement in a continuous rhythm that she relied on more and more these days. She kept running until her feet hurt, and her lungs burned. She stopped and tried to catch her breath but struggled. She had run hard. As she stood there breathing in and out, wheezing, trying to catch her breath she took in her surroundings.

I have no clue where I am; she thought to herself. She tried to picture her route, visualizing the turns she had taken. She looked back down the street she was on. Just then someone grabbed her from behind, putting a hand over her mouth and the other over and around her stomach.

Think, think she told herself but instinct kicked in. She dropped all of her weight and then pushed back really hard. Her attacker stumbled and lost his balance, he didn't go down but he released her then she spun around kicking her left leg out hard as she turned. He wasn't expecting that, she thought as her foot connected hard to his abdomen. She punched with her right and left fists quick and hard and watched her attacker pause, looking stunned. That second she turned and ran, sprinted as fast as she could. She did not stop or look behind her until she got to a few kids selling lemonade and cookies.

She came to a halt, panting, lungs on fire. "Mom — dad — where" she sputtered out in between gulps of air. The kids looked shocked, and the boy turned and ran toward the house. Moments later two adults came rushing out of the house. Jelena is still trying to catch her breath.

"My name — Jelena Cohert FBI — phone please" she paused "I live in Sunny Isle and I was just attacked on my jog, can I use a phone." The couple looked horrified but were eager to help. She called the local base and reported the crime "male, 6'0, white, blonde hair, short, muscular build." she spoke into the phone. He didn't have a mask on, she thought to herself. She instructed the officer to meet her at her house for the formal statement. She talked to the couple and realized it was a 10 mile journey back to her house, she had run into Great palm which was the next subdivision.

She took the gentleman's offer to drive her home. Where did he come from, was he on foot, how could I have missed him following me, who was he, he didn't have a mask that means he meant to harm, to kill me? These thoughts turned and turned around in her head on the ride back. As she pulled into her driveway, she looked at her house with dread. She didn't want to tell Dan. She got out of the car and thanked the man for the ride. Just as she was turning the knob a unie pulled up. She stood outside and gave her statement.

She entered the house and stripped her shoes off at the door. She walked into the kitchen for a glass of water, no wine, she needed wine. She poured her a glass and then sat on a stool by the island. She looked around and saw the kitchen clean, all the food put up with pots and pans washed. I need my phone, she thought. She went upstairs holding her glass and retrieved her phone from the charger next to the bed. She noticed Dan wasn't around. She went back downstairs and called Angela; they spoke in Spanish.

Jelena: girl, I just got attacked

Angela: ATTACKED I'm on my way

With that, Angela hung up the phone. Jelena placed her phone down on the island. As she drank her glass of wine, she wondered whether to go searching for Dan. The universe answered her question and Dan walked into the kitchen. He sat on the stool next to her and began speaking. She held up her hand to stop him. This was the moment, what was she going to do. Was she going to tell her husband she was attacked? He stared at her waiting for her to say something.

Jelena stared at Dan and said, "I don't care about the journal, I care that you don't trust me. On my run, I was attacked. Angela is on her way over to talk to me about it. I do not want to talk to you. Respect what I am saying and go back to whatever you were doing when I was gone.

She watched his features change from intensity to horror to sadness.

He looked at her for a minute after she finished talking. "I wanted to let you know I am on my way to my brother's house but Jelena I want to be there for you."

"Angela will be here for me," Jelena said.

30 minutes later Angela was banging at the door "¡chica, abre la puerta!" Jelena went to open the door and Angela stood there and looked her over.

"No cuts, no bruises, I'm fine" she said "now come on in, I will get you a glass of wine." They entered the house and went into the kitchen. Once they were both sitting Jelena told Angela the entire story from start to finish.

"Oh dios mío" Angela looked at her friend with sorrowful eyes.

They sat at the island and told each other about the office guy from the bar, Dan hiding the notebook, and the potential lead with the hacker. They stayed in for the night. They ordered a movie on demand and door dash. Dan walked into the living room with the coat and shoes on "Hello Ang."

"Hey Dan" she said. He looked at his wife with so much emotion in his eyes "I am on my way out Jelena."

She looked back at him and nodded her head.

Angela looked at her wide eyed "oh dios mio girl. It really upset you, huh?"

Jelena signed and looked at her "we just got into it because of the language thing, and now he is hiding things afraid he can't trust me to not look at it. Like I go snooping through his things" she threw her hands in the air, exasperated.

After a few more hours of food, movies and talking she watched Angela get in her car and drive away. She closed the door and glanced at the wall clock. She noticed it was just after midnight. Jelena went upstairs. She closed the bathroom door and ran herself a bath. As she soaked herself she ran through thoughts of her marriage. Jelena and Dan had been together for years. She wondered what so important and secret was in the notebook that he hid it from her. She lost track of time soaking in the water. Once in the bed she checked her phone, preparing to turn it on; do not disturb. She noticed a next message from an unknown number it read:

I missed you this time bitch, my mistake for underestimating you. WILL NOT HAPPEN AGAIN.

#

Dan arrived at his brother's house and knocked on the door. Two kids answered the door. One was an eight-year-old girl with curly blonde hair and the other was an 11-year-old boy with short dirty blonde hair "uncle Dan" they said in unison as they jumped on him.

"Hey kids" he chuckled as he hugged them.

"Okay y'all, get off your uncle Dan before you break him," said a woman rushing to the door. "Let him in the house at least" she giggled. The kids ran back into the house and his brother's wife came to the door to greet him.

He hugged her and said "hey Amy."

"Come on in Dan, your brother is in the den waiting for you."

Dan walked through the house and saw his brother and his brother's best friend sitting there talking. They rose when he entered and he went to hug his brother "Hey Drew" he said. He walked over to Jacob and the two shook hands. Once the pleasantries were done the three gentlemen sat down.

"Dan, you want a beer?" Drew asked his brother.

"Dan laughed "yeah, but I will get it myself." Dan got up and walked into the kitchen to grab a beverage.

"Why the laugh?" Drew yelled into the kitchen.

Dan returned and popped the cap on his beer. He took a long swig from the drink and swallowed it.

"So tell me what is going on brother" Drew said.

Dan looked at Drew and Jacob and told them of the two fights he had this week with his wife. When he was done, he looked at the two men in front of him. It was silent for a few moments and Dan said "well" trying to encourage one of them to say something.

"So let's take these two at a time," Drew says. "How do you feel about the first argument, with the language thing?"

"I feel she overreacted. But then she spoke in French, which turned the entire thing from being about her being too sensitive to know I am the bad guy. An uncomplicated way to solve the problem is to speak in English." Dan replied.

"Did you guys decide that you would learn each other's language?" Jacob asked.

"15 years ago" said exasperated

"But Dan" Drew said, sitting up in his seat, "you shouldn't have waited 20 years. That is the thing. It would even frustrate me. The two of you made this pack to learn each other's language. She learned French, you had no interest in learning Spanish, so you smiled in her face and did what you wanted. You didn't communicate."

"The only person she speaks Spanish with is Angela," Dan says, sitting with his back all the way back on the chair. "I know she has siblings and parents but I have seen none of them. So what culture" Dan said "is she trying so to hold on to? She has green eyes and blonde hair for God sacks,"

Jacob was sitting opposite Drew and Dan. he had his hands

clasped in front of him and had been watching until this point. He looked at Dan in disbelief. Jacob was a black man married to a black woman. He had known the brothers since they all went to the same preschool. Jacob's parents did not have a lot of money, but they always had enough to send him to private schools. Being a black man in private schools gave him early and intense experiences of prejudices, discrimination and racism. He has never known the brothers to be racist or engage in acts of discrimination. But he saw what Dan was saying here. "You married a white girl with a tan" Jacob said "and when she speaks Spanish, you don't like it because it reminds you that she isn't."

Dan got defensive and slid up to the front of his chair, pointing his finger at Jacob "how dare you" he bellowed "sounds like you are trying to call me a racist. I knew she wasn't white." Dan stared at him, ready for a fight.

Jacob looked at Drew "you can go back to the empathetic thing," he said looking at Drew "he is not ready to be honest."

Dan was up on his feet in an instant "Do not talk about me like Ia not standing right here"

Drew stood up holding his hands up in a stop motion "Whoa, Dan, why are you so mad?"

Dan looked at his brother with wide eyes "this man just called me a racist" he said raising his hand pointing it in the direction Jacob was sitting. "He is sitting there judging me, throwing his blackness in my face trying to unite with my wife based on some minorities stick together bullshit." Dan finished, and he was huffing and puffing, looking from Drew to Jacob.

Drew put his hand on his brother's shoulder, "I have kids, we do not yell and curse in this house. When my wife and I have a disagreement, we sit and have a conversation."

Dan took another huffing breath and turned and went back to the chair he was sitting in and plopped down, He sat all the way back in the chair with his arms parallel across each arm of the chair. Drew went back to sit in his chair. "Dan no one is calling you racist."

Dan looked at Jacob, scowling "You said yourself," Jacob began "that you have never seen her speak Spanish with anyone but Angela. You said yourself that you have never met her parents or siblings and that means to you she has no right to call that culture hers. You said yourself that she has green eyes and blonde hair. The only words that I added were that you lead yourself to believe you married a white girl. She looked like a white girl, talked like a white girl. She spoke like a white girl until she met Angela. Yea, she said she wanted you to learn Spanish, but you didn't take that."

Drew interjected before Dan could reply, "She told you when you guys dated that her culture was important to you, you told me that. She said she wanted you to learn Spanish. You said she started having you eat authentic Spanish food. You said she would take you to neighborhoods you have never been to, to go shopping at certain stores. Could it be so far fetched that who you saw and what you wanted matched, but the culture she was trying to get you to be aware of didn't so you just blew it off?"

"Well, what about her lying huh" Dan said glaring at the two other gentlemen. "What about that damn folder with fake names and grades in it? She is right too, huh?"

"Dan," Drew said in a soothing voice, "what does that have to do with you not wanting Jelena to speak Spanish around you?"

Dan breathed and rolled his eyes "fine, I don't want her

speaking Spanish because I don't like her doing or having things that have nothing to do with me. I'm white, I didn't want to learn Spanish then and I don't want to learn Spanish now. It pisses me off that after all this time she still speaks Spanish around me knowing I don't know what she is saying. I don't care that she knows French. I don't want to learn Spanish or anything else about that culture and I don't want my wife doing it either."

Jacob has been sitting just watching and listening. What he was hearing from Dan is that he is a prejudice, controlling individual. It has been suppressing his controlling tendencies because Jelena is an open partner. Communication is key with her and she is very open about everything else besides her job.

"Dan," Drew began "you know you do not control anything she does, right?"

"Aren't we married? I'm her husband, I should have control, and I have control."

Just then the three men heard a gasp from behind them. "How have I not known your authentic self all these years?" Rebecca, Drew's asked.

"Hunny, we are here just talking things out," Drew said.

"I know, and I kept the kids out of here to give you guys your space. I even took the kids upstairs when I started hearing the yelling. I had to come in here to listen when I heard…" she trailed off. "All these years," she began again "you were a wolf in sheep's clothing. Now that I see the predator, my children and I will not dine with the predator,"

Rebecca let out a tearful sigh, looked at her husband and turned and left. Drew put his head in his hands and sighed heavily. He brought his head up and looked at his brother.

"What" Dan said with his arms stretched out "what the hell

is she talking about"

"Dan, you sound very controlling," Drew said. "We don't believe in me controlling Rebecca, we are a team. That's what being married means"

"No," Dan said, "Married means she does what I say. She has for 15 years, why is it becoming an issue suddenly?"

Jacob spoke up "this is a conversation you should have with Jelena because it goes way deeper than 'we had a fight and I need to vent"

Dan glared at Jacob "you just think you know it all, huh?"

"Dan," Drew interrupted. "I have to go try to convince my wife that my brother can be around our children. Did you miss that part? Did you hear Rebecca say you are no longer allowed around our kids?"

"She is just being overdramatic," Dan said.

"No" Drew said more "she doesn't want our kids to grow up thinking a man is superior to a woman." Drew looked at him, willing his brother to say something to help his case. Dan stared at his brother with nothing in his eyes "I don't see what the issue is. Well, I know the issue with Jelena but I don't see what the recent issue is."

Jacob shook his head and stood up "It's been quite a night gentleman, I have to head home to make sure I put my kids to bed. I will see you all soon." Jacob shook Drew's hand and patted him on the shoulder. He then turned and looked at Dan. Jacob made a saluting motion and headed towards the door. Drew stared at his brother and wondered how they went their entire lives without him knowing this part of him.

"Dan, I think it's time for you to head out, it's after midnight."

"You're kicking me out? I came here to vent to my brother

and you're letting that - Jacob mess with your head."

"Dan, Jacob has been a part of our life forever. Why is there an issue suddenly?"

Dan shook his head in frustration, "I don't know," he said as he stood up.

Drew stood up and walked over and hugged his brother. Dan put up some resistance and first and then gave in and hugged his brother. Once the two released Dan made a beeline for the door.

Drew headed upstairs and stood in the bedroom door and stared at his wife. She looked up at him in disbelief, "how did I not know he had a different set of values than us? I would've never allowed him alone with my children had I known. How do I know what he has been saying to them when they were alone? I do not want my son growing up thinking he can dominate women, nor do I want my daughter to think she is not an equal. Yeah, she will have to work twice as hard but -"

"Rebecca, Rebecca" Drew cut her off and crossed the room. He sat on the bed beside his wife and hugged her.

"I have to call Jelena," Rebecca's muffled voice said.

Drew released her and looked at her "you think that's a good idea?"

"I would like to know. I wouldn't accept it at first, but I would want to know,"

#

Once Dan got home, he dropped his keys and coat off and went to the kitchen. He took a beer out of the refrigerator and gulped it. Dan headed upstairs and saw Jelena on the bed reading a book. "It's almost 1 am, you're not sleepy?"

"No," Jelena said without looking up.

Dan went over to her and kissed her on her forehead. He looked down at her and asked, "is something bothering you?" Jelena did not respond, and Dan rested his hand on her shoulder.

Jelena looked at him "is me not answering upsetting your need for control?"

Dan was taken aback. He took a few steps back and looked at Jelena. "What are you talking about?"

Jelena didn't respond and went back to reading her book.

"Jelena, what is your problem?"

"I do not have a problem, I am trying to read."

"There is something wrong with you. Can you put the book down so we can talk about it?"

Jelena looked up from her book, "you're asking me. I must call Rebecca and tell her about this one."

Dan's eyes narrowed and his mouth turned down in disgust, "Whatever Rebecca told you was a lie."

"That's how I know you're lying. Anyone who says someone else is lying without knowing what the other person is saying is a liar." Jelena put the book on the nightstand, turned her bedside lamp off and rolled over. "Bu-ena-s no-ches," Jelena said, enunciating every syllable.

Dan stood there in disbelief. He got this familiar feeling. The feeling when she did something stupid, and he wanted to correct her, let her know who is boss. The next feeling that came up is fear. Fear of pushing too hard and his world crumbling. 'A wolf in sheep's clothing' they called him. He was a very successful man because he could keep his tendencies in check. He didn't think there was anything wrong in the way he believed the world should go. He knew that everyone else would not accept it, so he hid it. Made a comfortable life for himself and this stupid Spanish thing would not ruin it.

Groundwork

Monday morning Cohert drove to HQ. Once she got there she went straight for her computer. She was early and no one else had gotten there yet, but she doubted they would work on the weekend. She needed to run a trace on that number that texted her. She went to the upstairs bedroom and grabbed her bag.

She went back downstairs and took her tablet and computer out. On one screen she had her police report pulled up, and she was in the FBI database on the other screen. She typed in the number that texted her and got no name or residence back. Must be a burner, she thought. She spent the next few minutes checking mug shots and trying to run down a store where the number could have originated. She was engrossed in her computer when Jonathan, Belle and Rodriguez walked in.

"Hey Cohort," Rodriguez and Belle said together.

She looked up from the computer and smiled at the both of them. Jonathan looked at her and smiled. They all gathered around the table.

"Okay so Rachel Macwire she has been hacking since she was 16 by self-report" Belle started "I haven't talked to the techs yet, I figured I'd wait for Clearweather" Belle rolled his eyes.

Angela tilted her head to the side "not going smooth between you two?" she asked.

Belle signed "He has this complex about him" he began, "it's like he is the only one on the team and if you disagree or challenge an idea, he can't handle it."

Cohert looked at him "I caught on to that," she said to him.

"Yea me too," Jonathan began, "when we were all talking things out and he told us to not worry about one scheme."

"Right," Belle said "I got a handle on it though."

The door opened and the FBI team got out their tablets and notebooks. Cohert closed down what she was working on and switched to the files on the Highworth Case. The police department guys came in and said their greetings as they sat down and got out their materials.

"Okay" Cohert began "Rachel Macwire is a self-reported hacker since she was 16 years old. She had done many jobs from minor social media hacking to hacking firms and bleeding them dry to releasing confidential information to the news. We can thank Belle for that rundown," she said pausing, looking through the room, then she continued "this weekend I came into the office based on a call that we had a suspect in custody. Macwire"

''Aka Slickey" Belle cut in.

Cohert continued "got caught by Johnson & Jones hacking into their systems. Rodriguez." She said, and all attention turned to her.

"When I was communicating with the company, I informed them of our plans and what we suspected that Highworth's plan was. They told me that they would up their security and put in traps to trap the hacker and notify the company. This is how Macwire got caught. She had already hacked into the dominant system and was trying to gain access to the accounts,

Price's account."

"Okay team" attention turned back to Cohert "this week we need to solidify the past cases. We need evidence processed, witnessed talked to, all the dots connected. We need that financial firm job put together more. That is the only weak part of our case. Go through old evidence if there is any physical evidence that needs to be tested, we have three weeks for a job that takes over two months. Rodriguez and Firestone you two are on that."

The detective and the agent got up from the table with their things and headed to a room with the boxes of materials they needed.

"We should take a trip to FBI headquarters to see if there is any evidence that we have that cannot be retrieved. Get copies and bring them back here."

Firestone looked at her with eyes of desire that that had gone so quick she questioned whether she saw it. "Brilliant idea," he said. He took a step back and made a wide gesture with his arms "after you."

She looked at him and they led the way outside.

Cohert continued talking about the suspect and how she needed to be questioned "she lawyered up this weekend, so make sure you do the T's and I's" she said looking at Belle and Clearweather. "Check in with the techs and see what they have discovered and check with Johnson & Jones. Collect any information you can that will nail the suspect and convince her cooperating is her best option, we need her to flip on Highworth. She has been convicted before so pull up those cases and become familiar so when you're talking to her we have established a pattern. Emphasize the apparent break from illegal activity and inquire why the sudden uptake."

Clearweather and Belle left and headed outside.

Once they close the door behind them Clearweather says to Belle "she said we could have the weekend. Wanted to show me up to your boss that bad."

Belle rolled his eyes "all I did was check the FBI database, which you don't have access to, and pulled up a summary of what we had on her. Let's split up the list. You go check in with Johnson & Jones. I will check with the FBI techs and we will meet at FBI headquarters to dig into her history and then pull her for our interview. You call her Lawyer and let him know the time to be present. Meet you at FBI HQ after lunch." With that Belle headed to his car without waiting for Clearweather to respond.

Cohert looked at Jonathan and Michaels "Okay guys I need you to do some groundwork and surveillance. We know Highworth's address, go put in work. Don't make yourself noticeable, we don't want her changing her plans any more than she will have to already."

Jonathan looked at her and said, "What do you mean already?"

Cohert sat down and looked at him "we have her hacker. So either she will get another one, or she will get the one we have out so she can use her. Either way, we need to be ready." Cohert looked back and forth at Jonathan and Michaels "I know surveillance work is not the best work but it is important work."

Jonathan and Michaels gathered their belongings off the table and headed out. Once sitting at the table alone Cohert said aloud "I have some leads to run down" got up, grabbed her things and headed out.

Cohert drove down to the neighborhood she needed to get to, where the store was located. She watched grand houses and manicured lawns turn to compact houses with brown dirt instead of grass. Her GPS signaled that she had reached her destination.

She looked at the convenient store and signed heavily. She took the key out of the ignition, grabbed her badge and headed into the store. The door chimed when she opened it, and she smelled stale, everything. She walked up to the cashier "Hello, Senior Agent Cohert from the FBI" she flashed her badge "I am looking for the owner or someone here most of the time." The guy in front of her looked to be in his mid-40s. His hair was long but thin. She saw he was missing teeth when we spoke.

The name tags on his dingy white shirt said Mike. "Well hello there" he said trying to eye her. "What can I do for you?"

She squared her shoulders "How many disposable phones do you think you sell?"

Mike turned around and went to the rack behind him with the cell phones. He seemed to count them and then walked back to her. "Truck was here the day before yesterday, we only get about 15 of them each week. Back there we have 7 left, so it seems we sold 8 already."

"Is there a way to tell whether the sales were cash or card?"

The cashier looked at her wild-eyed "lady I am not looking through the past three days of recipes!"

She looked at him and tilted her head to the side "can I?"

Mike reached under the counter and rumbled around for a minute. He came up with a black shoe box in his hand "Have at it."

She took the box and looked around "you got an office or something?"

Mike pointed to the back of the store "through there." Cohert walked back through the store to a little room off to the side.

Cohert opened the box hoping they organized it in some way. She saw a bunch of receipts clipped together with a binder clip. Thank God she thought when she realized they were at least clipped together by day. She began looking through the receipts. About 45 minutes later she had found all eight receipts with a cell phone on it. They had bought three of them with a card, she copied down the information. It's a long shot she thought as she put them into her bag. She replaced the paper in the box like she had found it and headed back out to the front. She handed the box to Mike, thanked him and headed to her car.

Cohert headed back to HQ. She hit the phone icon in her car and called Boss.

Boss: Cohert

Cohert: Yea boss, what do you think our chances are of getting a warrant to have Highworth's bank records released and can you hurry the exhumations along? I have two in the works, the other three are dragging their feet.

Boss: You know how those foreign banks operate, let me see what I can do. As for the dead bodies, how are the families taking it?

Cohert: They are fighting it, saying there is no need for the exhumations.

Boss: Wait and see if we find evidence on these two, then the other three are guaranteed.

With that he hung up. Cohert made it back to HQ and went upstairs to one bedroom. She pulled her computer and tablet out of her bag. She had to run down these receipts and see what handle she could get on Highworth's money. Cohert spent the better part of the day in a bedroom at HQ. She had her computer and tablet sprawled on the bed. She had two yellow note pads and a pen where she had scribbled her notes on. Her phone chirped, and she spread paper around to look for it. She picked it up and seen she had a message from Rodriguez

Rodriguez: we debriefing today?
C**ohert:** nope, see you all on Wednesday.
Rodriguez: 10/4

The next day Cohert had the addresses of all three men who used credit cards at the convenient store. The first name was Frank Kinckade. She was in front of a high-rise building, his apartment was D4. She gazed up at the building and wondered what would she do if this was him? How would she know if it was the same guy? She headed towards the building to herself trying her best to blend in. It took a few moments for someone to come to the door.

A tall guy with blonde short hair was looking back at her. "Agent" he said "How can I help you?"

She looked at him. How did he know I was an agent she thought? "Hello, I'm Senior Agent Cohert, you mind if I ask you a few questions?"

He looked at her with a glint of flirtatiousness in his eyes. "You want me to invite you in," he said, "what some vampire here to drink my blood." He then exposed his neck "bite and suck agent, bite and suck."

Cohert kept a straight face and asked again "mind if I ask you some questions?"

The man stepped back and did a wide gesture with his arms signaling her to enter the house. Cohert walked in and noticed the house looked odd for a man to be living here. There were feminine touches everywhere. The patterns of the house went well together. They were not matching, but they went well together. They were not black leather like some would think of most bachelor pads.

#

Mr. Kinckade led her into the living room and gestured for her to take a seat. She sat in an armchair that was so big she sank into it.

She relaxed in and crossed her legs. "As I mentioned I am Senior Agent Cohert, can you explain to me your whereabouts Saturday?"

He put his hand on his chin and looked up. "Hmm, Well I went for a run along my neighborhood, I took a trip to the grocery store. That's about it though."

"Where do you run?" She asked him not breaking the stare.

He looked at her then, "I run a little of everywhere dear, I like unfamiliar terrain."

"Where did you run on Saturday Mr. Kinckade?" she said with a no nonsense type of tone.

He looked at her with a glimmer in his eye "my, my, my, what a tone we have there. I do not remember where I ran on Saturday. I often go to the suburbs and run, so I can enjoy the scenery. The families, picket fences and the dogs. It has always been a dream of mine to be the family guy."

"Are you sure Mr. Kinckade, because you just told me you went for a run along your neighborhood?" Cohert said.

"No, I said – " Mr. Kinckade started and then trailed off.

Cohert took out her notebook and began taking notes. She looked back up at him expecting him to keep talking. However, it seems like her movement interrupted his answer. "You want a family, therefore you run in the suburbs" she prompted.

"Yes" he replied. Suddenly he doesn't like talking? She thought to herself. What spooked him, what did she say. "Mr. Kinckade, I'm sorry if I interrupted you by pulling my notebook out. I should've done that in the beginning."

"You didn't interrupt me," he said "next question."

She looked down at her notes, giving herself time to think of another question "About what time on Saturday did you go on a run?"

Frank looked up and to the right hmm she thought a sign of fabricating. Frank said "I like to go early in the morning, right as people finish breakfast, that's the best time."

Cohert jotted notes and also noted the sign of lying. She looked at him giving him time to finish, when he said nothing else she asked.

"About what time did you go grocery shopping?"

"Around noon," he said.

"How long did you spend running?"

"I run for an hour and a half." He would blow for blow with her, not stopping to think about his answers.

"Do you go grocery shopping in your neighborhood or the neighborhood you ran in?"

"I go in my neighborhood, just down the street."

"Okay," she said looking at him. "With an approximate 30 minute drive to any suburb you were at the grocery store down the street at noon. Which means you left your jogging neighborhood around 11:30 and started your jog around 10:00 am, going off the scenario you ran in another neighborhood and not your own as you stated at first is this correct?"

He looked as if thinking it over and she asked "What time did you leave the house Mr. Kinckade?"

"Uhh, uhh about well it would have to be 9:30 now wouldn't it?"

She looked at him, "I am not asking what it would have to be, I am asking what time did you leave your house?"

"I am not sure," he said, "I wasn't looking. All I know is that it was after breakfast."

"What time did you finish breakfast?" She asked him continuing with her rapid fire questioning style.

"I didn't set an alarm, I am not sure of the time."

"So you didn't look at the time until you got into the grocery store correct?"

He started looking irritated "no I didn't look at the time at all,"

She tilted her head "So how did you know you were at the grocery store around noon?"

He stood "It is time for you to leave,"

Cohert grabbed her belongings and had to slide out of the enormous chair she was sitting in. As she stood she looked at him and extended her hand "Thank you Mr. Kinckade, I will be in touch."

He grabbed her hand "I don't think so" he mumbled.

She looked at him, tilting her head to the side, "what was that?"

Frank used his body proximity to slide Cohert out of the door and slammed it. She noted the exit in her notes and then headed out of the building. When she got into her car she flipped through the pages of her notebook and put a star by Frank Kincade's name. Next on the list is John Parker. She typed his address into her GPS.

Frank peered out of his window. What do we have here he thought to himself? How did you find me Ms. Jelena? Frank looked at her as she looked through her notebook and started messing with the front console of her car. Could it be a case, or could it be you're after who attacked you. He left the window and went to the junk drawer in his kitchen. What led you to me he thought as he slammed the door open in anger. He searched through the drawers until he found the one he sent a text message through and broke it apart. He then dropped it in the sink and ran water over it. I will not tell Mr. Special Agent about this minor hiccup. Frank went back to the drawer and pulled out another burner phone and was about to text Jelena and then decided against it. He threw the phone back in the drawer and then pushed it closed.

#

Jelena pulled up in front of ranch-style house with an attached farm. She detested the farm animal smell. She exited the car trying not to inhale too as she headed to the front door.

She knocked twice and a redheaded tween, maybe 11 or 12 opened the door. "Yes" she said with a slight attitude.

"Can I speak to Mr. Mark Holmes?"

"And who are you?" Cohert pulled out her badged and showed the young lady "I am Senior Agent Jelena Cohert with the FBI."

The girls' eyes widened, and she took an involuntary step back. "Uh dad, FBI is here" and with that she shut the door in her face. Behind the door Cohert heard scuffling, and then the door jerked open. There stood a pudgy man with a receding hairline scowling at someone she could not see. He looked at her, and his face changed to that of a pleasant man.

"Ma'am, I am so sorry, I am Mark Holmes."

Cohert was sitting in a very dated living room across from Mark and a lady introduced to her as Sally Holmes. "Okay, Mr. and Mrs. Holmes I just have a few questions on an open investigation. Mr. Holmes, where were you this past Saturday?"

His eyes widened and then his poker face fell into place. "I can't remember, it was quite some time ago -"

"No, babe" the lady cut him off "you left the house around 9 and said you were going into town" Now he seemed mad. Hmm she thought does he fit the description of who attacked me. He is not 6'0 and blonde, so what is he hiding.

She pulled out her notebook and began writing "so you went into town and did what?" He took a few breaths and then his face fell back into place "Oh, that's right. I went to the market and then just sightseeing in the park."

"And you bought a burner phone" Cohert said. His wife's head jerked to the left to look at him.

"Why would you need a burner phone?" she asked him.

"It is time for you to leave now" he said as he got up off the couch. Sally stood up and stepped in front of him.

"You brought a burner phone when you were out doing what on Saturday?" Cohert looked up at him.

Mark looked at Cohert and said "I told you to leave " Sally took a step back and yelled "Girls, pack an overnight, we are leaving" and she walked away from him. Cohert gathered her belongings, said thank you and headed towards the door. Once in her car she looked at the few notes she had under his name. He did not fit the description like Kinckade did but there was something to hide there. "Marital drama" she said out loud as she typed in the last address.

Old and new crimes

Rodriguez and Firestone sat in the living area of the HQ house. "Firestone" Rodriguez said

"What have you found out about the firm thing?"

"What is with this Firestone thing, why can't we be Angela and Cassidy?"

She looked at him, "can we get to work, please? What have you been doing all this time?"

"Okay okay okay" he said "thanks to you letting me use your computer which to the FBI database I have more than we already did. Okay, so Highworth interviewed with the Security firm with a fake resume. She was hired her as a part of a team who got hired to hack into companies to see where their weaknesses are. She was only there for 2 weeks."

Rodriguez took out her tablet and began comparing what he was saying with what they already have in this section file. "How much money did she end up stealing?"

"She got just under 1 million dollars" Rodriguez looked up at him, eyes wide and gasped

"How did she end up stealing that much Dinero?"

"Yea she is good. The only way anyone found out is because there was someone at the school who saw the hack into the system and reported it. So when the firm got around to doing a search to check the resume, it came up that she was never a student there."

"Well" Rodriguez said "don't keep me in suspense."

Firestone did some clicking on the computer and turned the screen around. The screen showed several deductions from the firm's accounts over a two-week period. The amounts went from $100,000 up to half a million.

"Ah Dios mio, how did she take all this money with no one noticing?"

Firestone shrugged, "I don't know. It seems to me like she should have known she wouldn't be there for long. She was taking so much money someone had to notice. However, no one figured it out until her background check came back with the thing about the school. She got an email asking her to come to HR office, and she transferred the half a million dollars and got out of there."

Rodriguez shifted in her chair so that her right foot was underneath her "okay, so how did she get out once they became suspicious?"

Firestone clicked over on the computer a few times. "We have a lady exiting the elevator about 20 minutes after HR says they emailed 'Gloria'. This lady had black hair with bangs. Gloria's was a brown color with no bangs. This woman used crutches and had on oversized dirty clothes. We have witness statements from the front doormen saying she looked out-of-place coming out of the elevator. When she got closer, he noticed she had an odor and noted other people in the lobby making faces and staring. When she got within earshot, he just let her go through without further question."

Rodriguez looked puzzled as she stared at a blank spot in the room, "What are you thinking?" Firestone asked her.

"Well, what is the policy? Were the door men aware that she was wanted in HR for questioning? Do they stop people on the way out? I mean, why was there such an enormous deal with this person? It just makes little sense to me."

"We are setting a pattern," Firestone said, adjusting in his chair after putting the computer down.

"She is a con artist. We have a timeline of HR calling Gloria down to answer some questions. We can have them testify to that. Then we have a sizeable amount of money being transferred out of their accounts into an account overseas. Within minutes of that we have a female leaving the lobby so foul smelling that she wasn't stopped at the door. The doormen rarely stop and question however, the one I spoke to doesn't have a description, and he didn't pay attention because of the way she looked. He could only give a general description."

"Okay can we tie Gloria to Highworth?" Rodriguez asked him.

"The techs tie the hack at the University back to an ip name that they know Highworth has used." Rodriguez pumped her fist in the air "yes," she said "a link."

Belle walked into the FBI building and went up to his cubicle. He started off by checking to see if the techs put in their report yet. He printed off the report, and he glanced over it. All this technology stuff went over his head but the tech Gretchen liked it when he said something from the report when he came down answering questions. He saw something that talked about her computer being clear. He assumed that meant she had not been hacking anything. He picked up the paper and headed to Gretchen's office. "Hello Ma lady"

Gretchen smiled without looking up from her computer. He leaned over her chair and placed her report in front of her.

"Nope, do not butcher my report. I will just tell you what I found." she said with a chuckle. Belle smiled and sat half on the edge of her desk and half off.

"Give me what you got," he replied.

"Jones & Johnson put up a trap -"

Belle interrupted Gretchen "in English please" he said with a slight smile.

Gretchen raised one eyebrow "what do you mean 'in English', I always talk in English." She gave a little smirk and continued "Jones & Johnson put a program in their system that tracks anyone who enters, sanctioned or not, and gives a detailed description of the persons uhh electronic signature" she said trying to find a simplified way of explaining her findings.

"So once the suspect entered along with anyone else who enters, the company gets an alert." Belle held up his hand with his index finger sticking out, "Who is on the other end? Is there a tech or someone sitting at a computer looking into each ping they get?"

Gretchen swiveled her chair to face him and crossed her right leg over her left. "No, the head of IT for the company set it up so alerts are sent to his phone. He checks when he is alerted, however he just looks and see if the information giving matches someone at the company. When the suspect tried to enter he did not check right away however, when she tried to access the Price account a separate alert went to him and he activated the protocol to lock her out and also locking her system. Then he contacted the office."

Belle stared off, looking at the wall, thinking. "Do we have anything else on her?" he asked.

"Upon further research after Jones & Johnson sent us what they had we realized the same signature being linked to some old hacker crimes. Jones & Johnson pinged an address from the computer signal. When our guys showed up, there was only one person there we arrested her. Turns out Slickey aka Rachel Macwire is an old pro who got out of the game a long time ago."

Belle stood up straight "that means she knows Highworth" he looked at Gretchen "thanks doll" he said with a wink and headed to the conference room to see if Clearweather had turned up yet.

Clearweather was waiting in the waiting room in Jones & Johnson. He spoke to the lady at the front desk and she told him to have a seat. He heard the clacking of heels and looked up to see Jaime, as her name tag read, walking towards him. She reached to shake his hand, and he shook hers back "Right this way Mr. Clearweather" she said. He released her hand, and he noticed she had slipped him something. He stopped in misbelief as he noticed she had slipped him her number. He picked up his pace to catch up with her. However, right when he was close enough to speak she opened a door and said "Mr. Jones and Mr. Johnson will see you now" with a smile. He shoved his hands in his pockets and walked into the room.

Two men are standing on the opposite side of the room, behind a grand desk. Clearweather looks around and notes all the degrees and awards on the walls. He walks up to the man on the right and sticks out his hand. A brown-skinned man with a bald head returns his gesture. He is wearing an expensive-looking suit with cufflinks with DG embroidered on the side. Clearweather then turns his attention to the short white man to his left. He has on a button up white shirt and blue jeans. The men shake hands, and the one on the right offers Clearweather a seat. As they sit down, he introduces himself.

"I'm Derek Johnson and this is Steve Jones" pointing at his

partner "we understand you would like information about our recent hacker?"

"Yes," Clearweather replies "you have been in contact with my colleague Angela Rodriguez about our investigation into your client Ms. Price."

"Yes, we were notified that someone would try to hack our system. We put security in place and stopped the intrusion." Johnson replied.

"You stopped the initial attack —"

"No" Johnson interrupted we have stopped all attacks."

"Sir," Clearweather said through a deep breath, "the hacker we have in custody was working for a con artist we are after. We have put a wrench in her plan. So now she either will get her hacker out of our custody or get a new hacker. We have every reason to believe she will not abort her plan."

Johnson stood up "we have stopped the threat. Thank you for your cooperation in this matter. Have an enjoyable day."

Clearweather looked at him, stunned. He stood up and looked back and forth between both gentlemen. "The bureau will send over the right subpoenas for access to your systems."

Johnson went to protest, but Clearweather cut him off, "Thank you for your cooperation in this matter. Have an enjoyable day." With that, he turned around and walked out of the office. As he passed the receptionist he smiled and stuck his hands in his pocket, feeling the paper.

Out in the parking lot, Clearweather pulled out his notebook and wrote the conversation he had with Johnson & Jones and his observations. He started the car as he threw the notebook in the passenger side seat, "off to see Mr. FBI guy" he mumbled as he drove off.

Belle met Clearweather downstairs, Clearweather scoffed

and said, "I need an escort now?"

"I could go back upstairs and have you go through the visitor protocol or you can get over yourself and come on." Belle continued to walk without waiting for Clearweather to reply.

Clearweather rolled his eyes and decided his pride was more important and went into the visitor's line. 45 minutes later he made it through the line and went in search for Belle. He got upstairs looking at names posted on cubicles.

A blonde popped her head up "Can I help you?"

He smiled and replied, "I am looking for uhh Belle, I don't remember his first name."

"Okay, we have two of them but one is in an interview right now."

He stopped her "I am a part of the task force"

Her eyes got wide "yes, he is in the interview room three that way" she pointed. He thanked her and turned, pissed off he started the interview without him.

Clearweather rushes to the room and as he enters Belle is standing up shaking the suspect, and who is presumed to be her lawyer "thank you for your time" he says right before they leave.

Clearweather waits until they both leave and turns towards Belle ready to leave and he stands in front of him preventing his exit "Why didn't you wait for me!"

Belle looked up at him staring him in the eye "the lawyer did not want to wait. We set up a time for the interview, and then you had me waiting 10 minutes. The lawyer came out and said if we didn't start now he was leaving. Next time leave your pride at the door and you would have been up here 45 minutes go."

Belle walked past him, bumping his shoulder. Clearweather stood there seething. He pulled out his phone and called his captain.

Cross: Hey DC, what's up.

Clearweather: I need to be switched off by this team boss.

Cross: why

Clearweather told Cross what has been happening over the past few weeks.

Cross took a deep breath over the phone "this one is on you DC. You are a skilled detective who does brilliant work. You are the senior detective out of you and your partner. In this task force the senior is Cohert."

"I am not trying to run things" he interrupted.

"What wonderful sense does it make to have a task force of competent investigators and tell them not to investigate?" Clearweather stood up and began pacing in the interrogation room

"We didn't have information about it. In hindsight, they did well, but no one can fault me on telling them not to worry about it because it wasn't solid."

Cross raised his voice, "First off you cannot tell anyone anything you can suggest and converse. Rookie mistake telling investigators not to investigate. the only two who had no current task? As for today, if you would have walked in with Belle you would have been on time for the interview. Your pride caused you that moment. I am not taking you off the case. Wise up and deal with it."

Clearweather sighed "yes sir" and hung up the phone.

Belle looked through the one way glass at Clearweather with a smile on his face. That's what you get he thought to himself. He waited until he heard Clearweather walk past the room he was in and then left. The two met at Belle's cubicle and then they went to a conference room and compared notes.

Jonathan and Michaels sat in a black suburban across from Jane Stoneybrooke's house. They have already confirmed that Jane Stoneybrooke is Sandra Highworth.

"Surveillance is the worst part of the damn job "Michaels says.

"I haven't done it in so long," Jonathan started

"I forgot how much I hated it." Michaels chuckles and elbowed Jonathan "the big bad fed doesn't leg work anymore."

Just then a black van came up and Rachel Macwire got out and walked up to the house. Both of the men looked at each other, "I will call Cohert" he said as he pulled his phone out of his office.

Cohert: Come into the office first thing in the morning.

He stared at the text on his phone surprised she had already contacted him. Michaels looked at Jonathan "she said to come into the office in the morning"

"So do we keep watch or do we take the day?"

"How about we go get food then come back?"

"A little breaking the rules" Michaels chuckles.

Michaels put the car in drive and did a K turn in the street. They made their way out of the winding streets of the cul-de-sac and when they came to a stop sign, they saw a man and woman at a house garage looking like they were arguing. Michaels hesitated as he watched the scene play out. The man grabbed the woman; and she punched him in the face. That made the man stumble back a bit, but he recovered and jabbed twice at the woman ready for it and dodged it with ease. Michael's phone buzzed and both men's attention went to the message.

"We have to hurry" Michaels said. When they looked back up the man was shutting the door to the car.

"What about them?" Jonathan said.

"We have to go and she can handle herself, look she's already in the house." Jonathan shrugged and Michaels pulled off.

You cannot die on accident

I don't know how long it's been. The blood has rushed to my head but the lightheaded feeling has gone away. My ankles hurt now. I switch between letting my arms dangle and folding them across my chest, switching them when one way hurts too much. I tried to do pull-ups but I do not have enough energy. All I can do is dangle here looking at the three crackers that are out of my reach. I could not reach the water. I feel my stomach and ribs like there is no meat there at all, just skin. I wonder if anyone is looking for me, has anyone noticed I was gone. I sob. I cannot believe I still have tears left. I've been crying for two days, three days, how many days has it been? I remember stopping at my office before going to the last name on my list house. How did I get taken, how did he over power me. Oh my God, is that footsteps I hear? Why is the coming back, stay away? Or do I want him to come back. I am so hungry and I have not drunk anything since the last time.

I open the door nice and slow and let the creek echo. As I start down the stairs, taking my time I notice her water is untouched. Shit, she didn't drink it. I rush down the stairs. "You little bitch, why didn't you drink". I reach down and grab the water so most of the water spilled out of the glass. I went over to the crank and cranked her *up to my level and shoved the water in her mouth. "Drink, you think you will die before I am ready for you to die!" I stomp over to my work desk, throwing the glass down. "I can't believe that little bitch has drank no water in two damn days." I grab my six-inch blade and stomp over to her. I plunge it into her abdomen over and over and over. She is screaming but I don't hear the screams just sound coming from her. I feel her go limp. I jerked out of my rage and look at her limp body. "SHIT" I rush over and release the crank dropping her down to the floor. She is bleeding everywhere. "What have you done, what have you done?" I was not ready for you to die "See!" I shout at her "look what you've done you dumb bitch!"*

He is undoing my chains. He stabbed me so many times. He lifted me up and threw me over his shoulder. The blood gushed out of my many wounds. I hear him blaming me. Saying I tried to die without his permission. He goes up the stairs and to the front door. Are we going outside? I could escape. Who am I kidding I have, OW, please stop, all the bumping hurts. I hit the ground with a hard thud. A fresh flood of blood leaves my body. I keep bumping up and down; I try to roll over but I can't. "Stay still stop moving, you're making the blood come faster." I hear him yell. He sounds different now, angry. He has never sounded like this before. What does he mean moving, I don't think I'm moving "Damn potholes" I hear him say "Got the bitch bleeding all over my car?" I am in a car. The realization makes my body ache all over. I am overwhelmed by terror. Terror so intense it makes me forget all the stab wounds, forget the torture and violation I have suffered and then the terror leads me to blackness.

I pick up my phone and dial my cleaner's number. I tell her I need the deluxe clean and ignore her requests for further information "Just bring everything you have" I shout into the phone before I throw it across the front seat. I keep glancing back and see the mess she has made my backseat. "Fucking Bitch" I mutter. "It is her fault, all of this is her fault. If she just would have behaved and drank the damn water. Trying to kill herself before I am ready. I hit the brakes so hard the seat belt locks, and I almost gave myself whiplash. I pulled up next to a brush area that goes downhill. I get out and drag her out of my car "Damn girl died, on her own. All of this is her fault" where my last words as I rolled her down the hill. I pull out my phone and test done to the damn supervisory special agent.

Is something wrong?

Wednesday morning the entire team is sitting in the kitchen at HQ waiting for Cohert to arrive. Rodriguez's phone buzzes signifying she has a text message. She glances at it while the team continues to talk. "She just gave us our assignments yesterday, she said we had until Wednesday. Why would she want us back so quick?" Firestone says.

Michaels speaks up "nope, we saw the suspect Rachel getting out of a car going into Highworth's house."

"What" everyone says in unison.

Rodriguez says "I have the details, silencio" everyone stops and turns towards Rodriguez.

"The suspect is out of custody and someone posted her 2 million dollar bail. Now we know for sure that she is working with Highworth because Jonathan and Michaels saw her going into her house. Cohert wants us to go back to our assignments and she will see us Friday for a review."

"That makes little sense," Belle says. "Her call the first time made it seem like it was something urgent, a major break in the case. Why would she only not show up but send a text saying keep doing what you're doing?"

Clearweather stood up first "Well, this was a waste of time

and I have stuff to do." with that the group disbursed.

Rodriguez sat at the table for a minute and tried calling Cohert, she left a voice message "Girl, call me. You're acting loca. Is this some cry for help? Call me back."

She hangs up and looks to see Firestone standing in the door frame looking at her "What has got you worried?"

Rodriguez signed and shrugged her shoulders "it's just uncharacteristic of Cohert, that's all. I'm being tonta."

Firestone sits in the chair next to her. He leans over in the chair resting his elbows on his knees. "I do not understand what tonta means" he smiles as Rodriguez chuckled "you butchered that word."

Firestone chuckles and then looks at her. "You know her well. Listen to your gut." Rodriguez stands up from the chair "I'm getting way over my head. It's not like she has been kidnapped or something, something just came up. I am sure she will fill me in later."

Rodriguez smiled down at him and patted him on his shoulder as he walked past him. Once in her car she pulled out her phone and sent off a text: Call me girl.

Later that night Dan is in the kitchen finishing up dinner. He has his podcast playing in the background. Dan finishes up dinner just as his hour podcast show has ended. It is the second one he has listened to, and he walks over to his phone to the episode from his playlist. Dan gets his phone off and shoots a quick text to Jelena asking her if she wants him to make her a plate or put the food up. He hits send and then goes to the couch to watch some Netflix. He flipped through the movies, and then went over to the TV shows. The first row was the 'continue watching' section. We are supposed to be watching Royal Pains together, he thought as he lingered over the TV show. What the hell, she's not home, she will never know.

He clicked on the show and started his dinner. Dan reached down to grab his beer and realized he left it in the kitchen. He put his plate up and got up from the couch. Dan stumbled from looking back at the TV and almost ran into the island craning his neck. "Why didn't I pause it?" he mumbled.

Dan grabs a beer out of the fridge and grabs his phone off the counter. He notices no text or call from Jelena. Dan rolls his eyes and heads back to the TV, leaving his phone on the counter.

Dan wakes up to a loud bang, he jumps up dropping his plate off his lap sending all the scraps of food to the floor. He looked around disoriented for a minute. Picking up the remote he turned off the TV and cursed when he steps and stepped into something wet. Dan looks at the floor and realizes his plate fell "Damn" he says as he picks up the plate. He walks into the kitchen and drops the plate in the sink. Dan grabs his phone and a few paper towels and heads back into the living room. On the walk he checks and notice still no word from Jelena, but it is after midnight. He calls Angela. Angela answers the phone sounding breathless

Angela: Dan, what's wrong?

Dan: hey Angela, can you just tell Jelena to call me, she is not answering my b texts.

Angela sits up in bed and pushes her partner a little to give him the idea to give her a minute.

Angela: Dan I haven't seen Jelena since this morning at debriefing. You mean she hasn't called or come home yet?

Dan: I assumed she was at work, that it was a late night.

Angela: Mi Dios Dan this makes me worry. Maybe she is at the other -

Dan: The other what Ang.

Angela: Um, I have a place in mind. I can't give you details though FBI stuff. I call you in a few to let you know okay. Bye

Angela hung up the phone before Dan answered. She sat up straight in bed. Hearing Cassidy sigh as she dials another number on her phone. Cassidy tugged on her waist attempting to roll her over towards him. She swatted him with one hand while typing away on her phone with the other. "Stop" she said half distracted and half irritated.

"Come back to bed" Cassidy whined. She was about to respond and then Belle picked up the phone "Hello" he said.

"Belle meet me at the Warrington Ave house. Something might have — our gut was right. Something happened."

Belle replied "Got it." They both hung up Belle pulled up the Warrington house as Rodriguez was getting out of the car.

"Sorry for the delay, I stopped by HQ house first to see if she was there."

Rodriguez said out loud "Her car is right here. That is weird she -"

Belle finished "She wouldn't have left her car out in the open because Dan would drive by." Rodriguez tried the doorknob to the passenger side door. When the door opens, she looks inside. Belle opens the driver side door "Keys in the ignition" he notes. "Here is the garage clicker" she says as she pulls it out and opens the garage door. Belle backs away from the car to watch the door open.

As he is waiting for the door to open something shiny catches his eye underneath the car. He reaches down looking at a silver tube. He stands up and goes to the trunk of his car. He searches around for a minute and pulls out two pairs of latex free gloves.

He walks back over to where he was when he saw the silver tube. On his way, he threw Rodriguez a pair of gloves.

He gets on the ground to get a better look and realizes it is a lipstick tube. Now on his knees and halfway under the car, now he has a better view.

"Her purse" he says at the same time Rodriguez says

"The car." They both say "what" at the same time. Belle stands up straight and pulls out his phone and calls Boss.

"Sir, we have a situation. Cohert is missing we are at the Warrington house, send help please." The Boss replied "got it," and Belle hung up the phone.

"Her purse and all of its contents are under the car." He said as he put his phone away and looked over at Rodriguez who was crying. He rushed around the car to her "Angela, what is the matter?" he said.

"There goes the federal car. I knew something was wrong, and I did nothing." She turned and sobbed in his arms.

Belle stood there and comforted her. What am I supposed to say? He thought to himself. He knew saying something like 'everything will be okay' and 'it's not your fault' would not be the right thing to say in this moment. We all say those things on the job but deep down say it because they expect it of us not because we believe the words. All of that to say, Rodriguez would not want to hear those things. She would want honesty, even if the truth was grim "I'm not sure but we will find her" Belle said.

Rodriguez hugged him as she continued to sob into arms. A few minutes later they were still standing there, in the same position. Rodriguez had stopped crying, but she didn't move. She couldn't move, not yet anyway. She was content in the space she was in. It lifted the boulder on her shoulders.

She knew the boulder was still there. The one signifying her mistakes but she was not feeling its correct weight, not in this space. She felt good, and that made her feel uneasy. She shifted a bit and he released his hold.

"You okay?" He asked her looking down at her, not letting her go.

"I don't know, I just feel" she signed "I'm just -" unable to finish her sentence she started attempting to hold back her tears. Belle began pulling her back into his embrace. She hesitated causing her to resist. "Cut that out," he said in a low tone. That's all it took, and she melted back into her safe space.

Chapter Twenty-one

Yes, something's wrong

Within 45 minutes the house on Warrington Ave was swarming with law enforcement. SSA Jackson and ASAC Monroe are standing with the officers and agents trying to get a grasp on what had happened. A crowd had gathered. Rodriguez looks at Belle and Jonathan and asks, "What am I supposed to tell Dan?"

Belle hugs her again and says "Let's wait until morning to cross that bridge."

The MDPD guys walk up. Firestone looks at Rodriguez as Belle back up when the three officers' approach.

"Have you been crying, Angela," Firestone asks.

Michaels interrupts, "What the rundown?"

ASAC Monroe walks up to the group, extending his hand to each officer. "Hello gentlemen, I am Assistant Special Agent in Charge Oliver Monroe. You have already met Supervisory Special Agent Jackson. As we understand it Jonathan and Michaels witnessed an altercation between who we now believe to be Jelena Cohert and her attacker."

Michaels jaw dropped as he looked around. Behind him was the stop sign they were stopped at earlier that day. "You mean we saw Cohert get kidnapped? Why didn't she say she lived in the same area as Highworth?"

Jonathan spoke up "I knew, I knew where she lived, I knew this corner. I was so wrapped up in wanting to get some food and she had sent a text saying we would meet in the morning. When I saw the fight, I assumed it was domestic or something. Which makes little sense now because she knew how to fight?"

"And by the time we turned our attention back, when we were being indecisive, we couldn't see her. We just saw the guy getting in the car. I assumed she went into the house or something. But, I was also thinking about why I seen our hacker going into Highworth's house."

Jackson's eyes shifted back and forth when Michaels mentioned Rachel Macwire. I had to let her go, he thought. She knew too much, she could bring Sandra down. Plus, I asked her to break the law. What else was I supposed to do? Cross looked at him and then turned his attention back to Monroe. "No need to beat yourself up over the past, fix it and move on" he said matter-of-factly.

"Based on our team's eyewitness account and evidence at the scene, there was a struggle. Cohert fought with her attacker.

He subdued her somehow." Monroe said.

Michaels jumped it "this is the point when we turned away but she was matching him blow for blow. I honestly thought it was a domestic, and she took self-defense. It didn't look like FBI training."

Cross put his hand on his shoulder and squeezed. Monroe looked at Michaels and continues, "looks like she used her purse as a weapon at first and then fought him. Somehow he got the upper hand and put her into his vehicle-"

Michaels interrupted again, "A dark blue Ford F-150 I didn't get the license plates."

Monroe continued, "We have techs combing the scene. I need you in whichever teams Cohert put you in" he waited a second while they arranged themselves. "Rodriguez, you and your guy go find her laptop and tablet I'll give the override codes-"

"SHE WAS ATTACKED" Rodriguez yelled out. Everyone stopped and looked at her. "The other day, this past weekend or something. I don't remember the exact day she and Dan were fighting, and we were supposed to go out. She went on a jog that morning and got attacked by someone. The police report said-"

Now it was Monroe's turn to interrupt. "It was bad enough for a police report and it did not get reported?"

Rodriguez shushed him, waving her hands up and down and continued "he was 6'0 with blonde hair. When I went over her house, she said she was running and was so mad she ended up like 10 miles away from her house. She was ambushed and surprised by him, which made it so she gained the advantage. She then ran until she came upon some kids with a family and asked for help."

Monroe appeared angry as he looked as SSA Jackson "Why

wasn't this put through the proper channels?" Monroe did not give him a chance to answer. "Rodriguez, you and your guy find her. Belle, you and your guy stay on Highworth, I have a feeling she is behind this. Jonathan and your guy, I need you to go back to the tapes of Macwire. Look over the ones from the interview room, the jail phone calls and interviews. I need every word she said that is not privileged, recorded and analyzed. I am not telling you how to do your jobs" he paused and looked around "but I expect everyone in my office at 9 am with an update."

He looked at Captain Cross and nodded his head. The MDPD guys looked at Cross, Clearweather spoke up "he expects us to work all night?"

Rodriguez interrupted, "Firestone let's go, we have work to do." With that she spun on her heels, preparing to walk to her parked vehicle when she stopped in her tracks. Standing in front of her was Dan. She cried.

Monroe walked over to Jackson and picked up his head looking at Dan "do one thing right, go inform her husband." Firestone puts his arm around Rodriguez, and she sobs into his arms. Jackson walks over to Dan, "Mr. Cohert" he began "I am Supervisory Special Agent Jackson –"

"What is going on?" He interrupted "Why are you guys here, don't you work with Jelena?"

Jackson cleared his voice, "Mr. Cohert please. Agent Cohert is missing, they kidnapped her from this location –"

"THIS LOCATION!" Dan yelled what is this house, she works for the FBI how the hell did you let her get kidnapped? What are you doing to find my wife?" Dan broke down and began sobbing. He hit the ground on his knees hard.

Rodriguez came over and tried to put her arms around him, but he shook her off.

"You knew she has a whole separate life, I knew it. Which one is her husband number 2," Dan screamed as he got up scanning the crowd?

The MDPD guys came up to him "Listen man" Michaels began

"It's you," Dan interrupted. "You are the one fucking my wife," he accused.

Monroe stepped in, "She is a Senior FBI Agent Mr. Cohert. That is all the deception, she's not a trainer or a teacher. She is an active agent. Now stop accusing this task force of having sex with your wife before that becomes tomorrow's headline."

Dan stopped jerking around and looked from one person to the next. Breathing heavily, he said "what — no she — she taught classes to freshmen."

Rodriguez stepped towards him, "None of us teaches Dan. We all are active agents. Jelena is a senior agent." She looked up at him with sorrowful eyes. Dan looked at her with rage seeping from his eyes

"Find my fucking wife" he looked up at all the people standing in front of him 'all of you" with that he turned and walked away.

Rodriguez barked "Firestone lets go"

Once the officers and agents split up and dispersed Monroe pulled Jackson to the side. He had a stern look in his eye, "how many times did you fail at doing your fucking job since this investigation started?"

Jackson looked at him and huffed, "How was I supposed to know anything happened to her without her telling me?"

"Are you so disconnected with your team that she filed a police report and you didn't know about it?"

"How am I supposed to know about things happening on a

local level, she doesn't even live in Miami?"

"The incompetence here is amazing," Monroe said, raising his hands over his head.

"With all due respect, sir," Jackson began.

"No," Monroe interrupted "a key witness was just released on bail she should have never gotten. An agent has been kidnapped, and you didn't even know there was an issue"

"Agent's get hurt in the line of duty all the time" Jackson said.

"Get your team together Jackson before I give it to someone else." Monroe stomped off without giving Jackson a chance to reply. As soon as he got to his car, he pulled out his phone and called his father.

Monroe: Hola Papí

Deputy: Monroe, how's things going?

Monroe: Jelena is missing, kidnapped. There are signs of a struggle.

Deputy: How did this happen, who is to blame?

Monroe: I have Rodriguez and her MDPD partner on it. We debrief tomorrow at 9 am.

Deputy: I will be there.

Monroe hung up the phone and headed towards the bureau building. He needed to be in his office; he needed to find his sister.

Chapter Twenty-two

Where is Jelena?

Firestone and Rodriguez drove to HQ in silence. Firestone sat in the passenger seat playing with his fingers, hating the silence but not knowing what to say.

"I knew it," she said almost a mumble. "I knew something was wrong, and I did not act on it."

"What would you have done?"

"INVESTIGATE" she yelled, "I would not have gotten into bed with you. My best friend was being abducted and god knows what else and I was with you" she spit out the last few words.

"If I need to be the one you blame, I will take that on," Firestone said in a calm voice tone.

"You are to blame" she was sobbing now "you told me to let it go, you made me doubt my instincts" Rodriguez swerved and pulled over. She opened the car door, got out and slammed it shut. She began speed walking, almost running towards a wooded area that was off in the distance of about 500 feet away. Rodriguez tripped because her legs were moving so fast, but not fast enough at the same time. She didn't have time to hit the ground before enormous arms grabbed her and wrapped around her. She sank to the ground into these enormous arms and sobbed. Firestone and Rodriguez sat there, in the grass in front of a wooded area for so long he lost track.

"Alright let's go" Rodriguez said as she picked herself up off the ground. She whipped her hands on her pants, and they whipped her face.

Firestone stood up "You ready to go?"

She began walking towards the car, "we have work to do," she said.

Once In the driver's seat Firestone asked "where to."

She checked her phone, and it was 2 am I wasted a lot of fucking time crying on the ground she thought. "Let's go to HQ and look into her tablet and see if her laptop is there. I will text Monroe and get her password so we can look at where she has been at any computer."

Firestone looked confused, "wouldn't we need the actual computer?"

"Nope" she said trying to sound cheerier "we always save to our individual clouds so we can get to our information from anywhere"

He nodded. They pulled into the HQ house and Rodriguez headed upstairs. She went from bedroom to bedroom looking for Cohert's bag. The last bedroom she was in she came across the bed filled with notes and yellow pads. She saw a bag in the corner and walked over to it, "Firestone" she called. Rodriguez pulled a laptop and tablet out of the bag and set it on the bed, careful not to mess up the papers.

Firestone walked in and looked around "what the hell" he mumbled.

Rodriguez tossed him the tablet and pulled out her phone "I'm texting Monroe."

Firestone sat in the armchair at the foot of the bed. She opened the tablet and looked at the login screen.

Rodriguez grabbed her phone when it buzzed. "Username is Cohert.JelenaSA and her password is JCARB5518!!." She said as they both logged into the devices they had. Firestone got busy searching the tablets history. Rodriguez sat on the bed and began looking through the paperwork as she waited for the computer to load.

"She was tracking down burner phones, it looks like"

"Yeah" Firestone said "I have three addresses looked up on here Frank Kinkcade, Mark Holmes and Tyler Malcolm." Rodriguez looked through the paperwork.

"Here goes a number written 555- 654 -4849 and a police report number. Wait, her police report, right? What other police report would she be looking up" As the computer signed in, she opened the history tab. She clicked on some of the most recent things open.

"Yes, she had her police report open, and she ran this number." She continued going through the pages. "Okay, what happened when she was attacked?" Firestone asked.

"She went running one day" Rodriguez began "she had a fight with Dan and needed to relieve some tension. She ended up running so far she ended up in another neighborhood before she realized where she was. When she stopped to catch her breath, she was attacked. She fought back, and it surprised him he knew how to fight. Once she got a shot, she took advantage of it and ran until she found a family who would help."

Without looking up from the tablet Firestone said, "So this guy tried to take her once, he has been watching her, but underestimated her ability. Which seems weird because if he had been watching her he knew she was FBI"

Rodriguez stopped what she was doing and looked at her. Sensing the change he looked up from the tablet "Because she is a girl" she said "yea she is FBI but most guys think that girls only have fighting skills in TV and movies, not in real life."

"Okay, so" he began as he rubbed his chin "she got enough of an advantage to turn and run. She filled the report, only because she had to ask the family for help."

Rodriguez jumped in, "Right, because she didn't go through the proper FBI protocols for reporting. She wasn't planning on reporting it, but since she needed help from the family, she had to get the police involved. When she told me she hadn't even told Dan yet. I'm not sure if he even knows now," she said.

Firestone kicked his shoes off and put his feet up on the edge of the bed. "Okay, you know her best, did she drop it or run the lead herself?"

"Herself," Rodriguez said almost "but wait, what lead? How did she jump to burner phones?"

"We need either her phone or phone records to confirm, but I assume the burner number contacted her."

Rodriguez went typing on her phone "I asked Monroe to get a copy of her phone records," she said. "Okay, if we are going under the assumption that the burner phone contacted her and that's why she ran the number. How did she get the three names?"

Rodriguez ran the phone number again in the database. The phone came up as a burner phone in a certain shipment. "Okay so she got that phone was shipped from the Timid Company."

Firestone picked up his phone as he asked did Rodriguez have a number for the company. He called the number gave his credentials so he could speak to someone in charge. He spent a few minutes on the phone. Rodriguez was looking at him. And then her phone buzzed. She picked it up and read it. Firestone ended the call and looked at her "so the guy was a little irritated at having to give this information to another FBI agent. The company has a database of the model numbers and phone number assigned to each phone. That phone was shipped to a convenience store at the other end of town."

Rodriguez looked up from her phone "next logical step would be to go to the store and see if there are any records. Also, Monroe has her phone in evidence and sent me what the burner phone sent her. The number texted her saying he wouldn't underestimate her again."

"So there is our connection," Firestone said. "She got attacked and then received a text message. She took the phone number, ran it and called the company to get an address to the same convenience store."

Rodriguez jumped up energized, "So the next logical step would be to go to the convenience store and look for records. She got her three names from there and then she went to interview each of them -"

Firestone interrupted her "okay, hold on" he said slowing her down. "Let's start at the beginning one at a time." Firestone took a small notebook out of his breast pocket and wrote timeline on the top of the paper. "What happened first" he asked Rodriguez?

"She got attacked while running in a different neighborhood." Rodriguez said as she sat back on the bed. "The next thing that happened was her receiving a text message from a burner phone."

Firestone wrote that down and then looked up at Rodriguez, urging her to continue. "Then she researched to find out where the burner phone was sold. That led her to step three going to the store."

Firestone stopped her "Do we have her notes of that interview?" Rodriguez looked around at the papers and notebooks she had around her "nope she doesn't."

"So that means we have to go back to the store and see what their conversation comprised."

"We know she got the three names from the store"

"Nope," Firestone interrupted "we assume that she doesn't have any notes remember?"

"Okay so let's go to the store and interview the workers there." Rodriguez jumped up and was heading to the door when Firestone jumped up and stopped her "Where are you going?"

Rodriguez looked at him in disbelief, "What do you mean? We have things to do. We have to go to the store and talk to the cashiers and managers."

"Angela, it's 4 am" Firestone said.

Rodriguez stood there stunned for a moment. "Well, we have a debriefing with Monroe, he is the Assistant Special Agent in Charge, and ya know my bosses, bosses, boss. We can't just sit around. We have to do something, time is money, they have kidnapped her Firestone!" Rodriguez shrieked.

Firestone put his hands on her shoulders and squeezed, "We cannot go talk to anyone at 4 am. We will have to wait until after the briefing to follow up with anyone. All we can do now is organized our affairs. Come up with a plan so we are running. The more prepared we are, the faster we can work."

Rodriguez' shoulders slumped, and she took a step back. She sank on the bed and sighed heavily. She looked up towards the ceiling. No tears, no tears, and no tears, she said over and over in her head.

"Crying is okay" Firestone whispered.

"No" she said, "It's not. I've cried enough." and just like that the floodgates were opened. She sat there and sobbed. How could I have missed this, she thought? "Tienes que superarlo." <you have to get over it> she said to herself. She climbed back on the bed and for a few more hours they got all their information together, working until it was time for the debrief.

Dan arrived home and slapped the door. He looked down through this house. "My wife, someone kidnapped my wife" he said aloud a few times. Saying it to make himself believe it. He went through the house in search for his phone. Once he found it he called his brother.

Drew: Hey Dan

Dan: I told you, I told all of you.

Drew: What are you talking about?

Dan: Jelena got kidnapped! She lied about her job she was an ACTIVE agent. She was in the field shooting at people and chasing a serial killer. And now she is kidnapped, and the FBI has no clue where she is. If I would have known where she was and what she was doing, like was supposed to happen in the first place, this would not have happened."

Dan finished his rant, huffing and puffing. His brother sat on the phone in silence, not saying nothing. Dan yelled into the phone "DREW DO YOU HEAR ME" then Dan cried. "Drew —- my wife —- she's" he couldn't finish. He slumped on the floor, crying. "Dan' Drew said through the phone "I am on my way."

there was a knock on the door. Dan didn't know how long he spent on the floor. He didn't have the energy to unlock the door. The knocks got louder "Dan it's me, open the door" Drew bellowed from the other side of the door. Dan picked himself up off the floor,, and shuffled to the door. Not having enough energy to pick his feet up off the ground. Once the door was open Drew got to work. Helping Dan get to the couch where he collapsed like his skeleton left his body. Then Drew headed to the kitchen and rummaged around a bit until he found the ingredients he needed. He pulled chamomile tea packets out of the cabinet and put them on the island. He went back to looking through the cabinets and pantry for honey and hops.

He found the honey in no time but was having trouble finding hops or any ingredient he could make into the sleep remedy. Drew came across a drawer names herbs. He opened the drawer and began moving the baggies of individual herbs to the side. He found a bag that said lemon balm. Caught his eye because in the label next to the name it said 'not for cooking'. He took out his phone real quick and Googled the name. "Sleep remedy" he said aloud and followed the directions on how to make tea with the herb, he then added honey and went back into the living room to his brother.

Dan was lying on the couch scrolling through his phone. He started laughing at something he saw. Drew walked closer with the mug. Once he was close, he tapped Dan on the shoulder. Dan craned his neck around and looked at Drew as if he didn't know he was in the house "Drew" he said loud and full of euphoria. Dan sat up on the couch and slid over giving Drew a place to sit. "Look at this" he said half laughing "it's hilarious." Dan leaned over trying to show Drew the phone. Drew took the phone and handed Dan the mug. Within 15 minutes Dan was asleep.

Drew laid his brother down on the couch and went over to the deep chair to sit. He pulled out his own phone and looked up Jelena's name. He didn't have to add anything else in the search box because the first headline 'FBI Agent Kidnapped on the Case'. He read through the article. Once he was finished, he signed and looked at his brother. His phone buzzed. He went to swipe ignore and realized it was his wife. "Drew, you didn't call to let me know everything was okay so now I'm envisioning worst-case scenarios" Rebecca said panicked into the phone.

Drew signed again, "He was bad when I got over here. I made some tea that put him to sleep. Jelena is an Agent Rebecca."

"You mean Dan was right about her hiding something about her job?"

"Big time" Drew said. Dan stirred, and Drew stilled a moment. When he resumed speaking he lowered his voice, "she is some hot-shot FBI agent who tracks down killers."

"Okay but what happened today. Why did you rush over there, because he found out she has a different job?" Rebecca said confused.

"someone has kidnapped her" Drew said as a matter-of-factly.

Rebecca gasped, "by a killer? A killer has her Drew" Rebecca said sounding like she was crying.

"I don't know" Drew said rubbing his forehead with his index and middle fingers "all I did was a Google search"

"I'll just get on Google then" Rebecca said. She said goodbye to Drew despite the protests and hung up the phone.

Find my daughter!

At 9am Thursday morning the task force was in the bureau building in a conference room waiting for Monroe to arrive. Everyone sat around the table making small talk except Rodriguez. She had her notepad and pen on the table, looking at a blank spot across the room. She was seated in between Firestone and Belle. Belle reached over and squeezed her hand. She looked at their hands and then up at him. She smiled and mouthed "te amo." Belle winked and released her hands. Firestone sat to the left of her watching the exchange between the two. He was just about to comment when the doors opened and in walked Assistant Special Agent in Charge Monroe and some other guy he didn't recognize.

"Hello" the man said getting right to business "I am Deputy Director Dominguez.

Firestone's eyes got wide, and he looked around the room. The Deputy Director continued

"This may seem like an enormous fish in a little pond scenario. I am not saying Monroe cannot do his job. To provide full disclosure, Jelena is my daughter and Monroe is my son. That information will not leave this room," he added. It shocked the crowd of agents and officers. Displaying their surprise and through facial expressions.

Everyone except Rodriguez, and this caught the attention of everyone in the room. Belle looked at her and she responded "she's my best friend, I knew" very.

Dominguez cleared his throat for attention. "We have assigned Jackson elsewhere because of his misgivings on this case. You will report to Monroe. What do we have on Highworth?" he said and then looked around the room waiting for someone to speak up.

Belle began, "Johnson & Jones informed us that they have moved the auction up. They are now having it August 25th."

Clearweather jumped in "When I went to interview them Johnson was unwilling to cooperate. He thanked us for telling him about the attack and then kicked me out. I had a feeling Jones wasn't on that same page though. I contacted him and told him that she would not abort her plan. When Belle and I followed up both Johnson and Jones informed us that they got Price to agree to move the auction up. We hoped that without her hacker, this would make her make mistakes."

The room moaned and groaned. A few people rolled their eyes and Dominguez spoke up "what am I missing?"

Monroe responded, "Sir, we have her assets frozen. We went into the bail hearing confident they would not release her. The judge set bail at $200,000 -"

Dominguez interrupted, 'Which is a lot for someone with no money."

Monroe continued, "she got bonded out"

Dominguez was taken aback a little. "So she is free? That information is public knowledge. Who bonded her out?"

Monroe looked at Belle and Clearweather. Clearweather looked at the high ranking agents and said, "the office is closed at night. It is the first thing on our to-do list though."

"Okay, remind me again why we are waiting for a wanted woman to commit another crime before we arrest her?" Dominguez asked.

Monroe responded, "they deleted her out of our system, sir."

Dominguez "But you have built your cases back up off of what we have in the archive, right?" Monroe nodded. "So arrest her! Unless we are waiting for this final theft to add to the case?" Dominguez asked?

Rodriguez spoke up "Jackson told Cohert that we could not arrest her because they hacked her out of our system. So we had to rebuild cases and wait for her to commit another crime to arrest her. That is the information she gave up at our first briefing"

Dominguez raised his voice, "you idiots, does that sound true to you?"

Everyone sat there, no one daring to be the first to speak "Sir, Jackson came to me and let me know a tech came to him and notified him Highworth was back in Miami. This was after Jackson was notified of the breach that wiped her from our system." Monroe said.

"Why weren't you notified? You know what, bring this tech up here. You go!" Dominguez pointed to Jonathan, and he left the room. Dominguez turned to Monroe and said through clenched teeth, "it's starting to sound like you don't know how to run your agents. This entire team was told that they couldn't arrest a wanted felon!" he said with a shout. Rodriguez averted her eyes knowing what was coming. She remembered Jelena telling her now her father could get.

Monroe stared up at his father. In these eyes "I thought they got a tip on her whereabouts, that she was in Miami to steal Price's money after the auction. They presented it to me the best plan would be to catch her at the auction and arrest her there. I was unaware he was lying."

"Incompetence" Dominguez yelled.

Monroe averted his eyes and said in a low tone, "incompetence."

Clearweather leaned over to Firestone and whispered "sucks to have your boss and your dad be the same person huh?" Firestone raised his eyebrows in return but didn't speak not going to unleash that on me he thought. Michaels sat on the far end of the table with his head on his phone. He looked up and seen Monroe's eyes. There were no down in submission. They were down to hide rage.

Jonathan came back into the room with a tech. His name tag read Steven. He was about 6'0 and well built. He had a confident look on his face until he seen Monroe and Dominguez. He stood at attention and nodded toward each man "sir" he said after the nod.

"Have a seat" Dominguez bellowed.

He sat in one of the empty chairs, next to Michaels. He noticed the officer with his head on his phone and his stomach fell. I am in trouble, he thought.

"How did you know Highworth was back in Miami?" Dominguez asked.

"I uhh, I had a setting-" Steven stuttered and then silent. Dominguez stared at him. Steven stared back up at him for a few moments and then slouched in his chair.

"Jackson told me to keep a tag out on the recognition program and let him know whenever I get a hit."

"How long ago' Dominguez bellowed

"Uhh last year sometime."

"How did you figure out she was no longer in our system?"

"I caught the breach. The hacker was good, so I wasn't able to lock him out before he erased her from our databases. I notified my supervisor and followed all the right protocols."

Dominguez looked at Monroe, "is there a team put together to find this hacker?"

Monroe nodded "yes sir."

Dominguez looked back at Steven, "when you got a hit on Highworth, what were your orders?"

Steven slouched in his chair even more "tell Jackson" and then he whispered "and only Jackson." Dominguez looked furious. "You're dismissed" he told Steven. Steven got up and exited the room. Dominguez stood there angrier than he could ever remember. "So I need to know who bonded our suspect out. Belle and -"

Dominguez looked at Clearweather and Clearweather replied, "Clearweather sir"

Dominguez continued, "Clearweather go run down that lead." the two gentlemen left the room. Dominguez turned to Rodriguez, "Where is my girl?"

Rodriguez began, "She got attacked this weekend and fought the attacker off. We assume he had been following her because one, she was attacked when she was running in a different neighborhood than where she lived and two, he texted her after the fact with a threat. However, he just tried to grab her and was, according to Jelena's notes, unaware she had combat training. That would lead us to believe if he was following her he didn't do a wonderful job. She followed up on the text messaged and ended up with three names but she only interviewed two, Frank Kinkcade, Mark Holmes. She has notes on both the two men. On our to-do list today is interview the store clear and both suspects."

"Okay" Dominguez said relaxing a little but "run them down quick come back with the update. Dominguez then turned to Michaels and Jonathan, "What were you two doing?" he asked.

Jonathan replied, "we listened to the interview tapes and jail records for Macwire."

Michaels jumped in, "And there is a definite link between Macwire and Highworth. The phone records from the jail, so many conversations between Macwire and Jane Stoneybrooke. We have already established Stoneybrooke is Highworth. Macwire told 'Stoneybrooke' that since she got her caught she needed to get her out of this mess. Stoneybrooke explained she couldn't use her money for bond because she didn't have enough transferred over. She said she would ask her dad. On a separate conversation Stoneybrooke told her dad would post bail but don't tell anyone who did it. They have a vague conversation about a 'party' still being on but they moved it up to August 25th, so they had to go 'shopping' soon."

Jonathan spoke up "but it makes me wonder why they were they being so vague about the 'party' being moved but not about posting bail?"

Monroe answered, "because she is thinking we will go look for Jane Stoneybrooke's dad. Do we know if she is a stolen identity or an alias?"

Michaels wrote on the pad in front of him "nope, but it is on the to-do list next to find out who posted bond but I guess Clearweather and Belle got that."

Dominguez spoke up "so you two go handle the alias angle and report back ASAP."

Those two left the room and Dominguez took a seat. Monroe knew where this was going and he sat down.

"Jackson has a lot of secrets Oliver, seems like he is playing both sides of this team."

"I gave him the clearance for the task force sir, but I kept out of it until I heard they had taken Jelena." Monroe replied.

"Have you been following leads?" Dominguez asked.

"I have been looking through the files and notes Jelena has been uploading to get familiar with what's going on."

"I need you to go through Jackson's cloud. Do it on his desktop though, so you have access to things he is saving in unique places. Figure out what's going on."

"Yes, sir" Monroe responded.

Dominguez put his hand on his son's shoulder "te amo yo hijo."

Monroe smiled and stood to leave the room.

The plan has changed

Macwire wakes up Thursday morning in a plus bed. She stretches out and then cuddles back together, loving the way the cotton sheets and pillows feel around her. She has been on a concrete slab with a two inch nothing in between for the past few days and it sucked. I will soak up all the guilt she is feeling, she thought. She laid in bed and sat there enjoying being in the present. There was a loud bang at the door and then it opened.

"Get up girl" Sandra said with a southern drawl "we got work to do." She came over and plopped down on the bed "The auction has been moved up, you got caught in the system, Danielle knows my and Jake's real names. This entire plan is going bad, I just need to abort -" she stopped when Slickey put her hands up in the air.

"So you will not go through with it?"

"How," Sandra said "you can't even get into the system remember?"

Slickey sat up and crossed her legs one over the other. "I know" she said "and I'm still trying to find a way around that."

Sandra threw her hands up in frustration and fell backwards onto the bed so that she was lying flat on her back. "What am I going to do?" she asked and then put her hands over her face.

"We can get back on the whole Danielle knows your actual name thing."

Sandra lifted her hands and peeked at Slickey and then put her hands back over her face. "She figured it out at the BBQ. I don't think she suspects anything about stealing her money. She knows we are lying or at least hiding our true identity."

Slickey looked down at her and then flopped back onto the bed to match her position. They lay there in silence for a minute. Slickey speaks first, "I have an idea," she whispered.

Sandra dropped her hands to her sides and stared up at the ceiling. After a few seconds of silence Sandra said, "Well."

Slickey turns to her side and props herself up on her elbow. Looking at Sandra she says "If I get can get into their system from the inside. I can hide in there and interrupt the money transfer while it is a process" she said and then waited for Sandra to reply.

"I'll bit" Sandra said "explain"

Slickey sat up in the bed and crossed her legs again, sitting facing Sandra. "Okay, so you said one we are at the auction the money gets transferred into Johnson & Jones's account. Then at the end there is a 30 minute transfer window., we were supposed to get to the money before they started transferring the money to Danielle Price now let's have the money transfer into your account instead of Danielle Price's and no one figure that out until the transfer is complete."

"I have two questions, one, how will no one figure out the account is different. Second, you cannot hack the system again, so how are we even going to pull this off?"

"I can spoof it" Slickey says getting more and more excited. "I can spoof the system so that someone looking at it thinks everything is normal, and it will look normal too. They will find out when the transfer is done. So we need to make sure we are long gone."

Sandra turned on her side facing Slickey, resting her weight on her elbow. "So they will trace everything?"

Slickey looked down "Yea, once someone investigates they will tell that it was me who hacked it and that the money went into your off shoes account."

"I have to leave Miami anyway," Sandra said "daddy's orders" she takes her free hand and does a mocking salute. "You have a life and stuff now. You're just going to leave?"

Slickey looks at her "I am being charged with a felony. The government will not give me two get out of jail free cards. I am going to prison, federal prison," she choked out.

Sandra sat up on the bed and crossed her legs facing Slickey. She leaned forward and put her hands on Slickey's shoulders and squeezed. "I am so sorry that I ruined your life" she said with tears welling in her eyes. She looked up at the ceiling and blinked them away. "I had this planned out right" She dropped her hands and put them in her lap. "My dad was supposed to be making sure I didn't have to worry about the Feds. You shouldn't have gotten caught. Now you have to live a life like I do." Sandra trailed off and looked away.

"A life like you do," Slickey said, "You mean the wonderful life you do, right? You have an unimaginable amount of untouchable money. You travel the world living in luxury. I would love to live like you."

Sandra looked at her smiling. "Do you have a favorite grocery store Slickey? Or a coffee shop you always go to? Do you have a book club or girl's night? Do you have a boyfriend or at least a steady fling? I can't afford to have any of those things. Nothing deep, nothing meaningful. No girls' nights or movie dates. No sleeping over with breakfast in the morning. I can't make any ties. Or if I do it's Nina, or Amanda who does to the coffee shop every morning and flirts with the manager. I have to have different likes and dislikes. Unique styles, careers, jobs. My life may seem luxurious, but it is no way to live."

Slickey stared at her in silence for a moment. "Well, if we will do this, I have no other choice. If I stay I'm caught."

Sandra looked at her "I'm sorry doll." Sandra said again.

"Okay, so are we doing this or not?"

Sandra sighed, "I can back out. I leave Miami like daddy wanted and find another big score."

Slickey glared at her "So I ruined my life for nothing. Bullshit. This is want I need you to do. I will give you a flash drive. You need to put it into the computer of the head tech guy's computer at Johnson and Jones. Once you do that give it 30 seconds and then take it and flush it down some toilet. Once they have downloaded my program, I can access the sight without detection and switch the account information. I will create a dummy with all of Price's information so that whoever looks at the accounts will see Danielle's price like nothing has changed. Can you do it?" Slickey asked.

Sandra looked at her and sighed. "Done" Sandra said and got out of the bed.

Sandra headed through the house to the kitchen where she found Jake. He was over the stove top cooking, and she stopped just to stare at him. My perfect life, she scoffed to herself. Her perfect life would be here. In Miami with Jake. Her dad wouldn't be an asshole. She shouldn't be this weak girl who got over on people to make herself feel worthy. She would be worthy, in her dad's eyes, in Jake's eyes. She wouldn't be - before she could finish her thought Jake turned around and smiled at her

"Hey, how long have you been standing there?"

"We have an alternative plan?" she said.

Jakes eyes widened, "so we are still doing this despite the whole Slickey thing? Oh, and talking about legal things. I was online looking through Facebook and came across an article on you."

Sandra sighed a bit "there are always articles on me, I'm exceptional." she said with a slight smile. Jake walked over the counter to grab his phone, opened Facebook and went to his saved articles as he walked over to her. "This is also a reason we should abort"

Sandra read the article, and her face turned deep red. Jake stared at her "so who told you that if they erased your information out of the FBI's system they could no longer arrest you, because they lied."

"My guy, Mike, he is the one who got the IDs for us. He told me the police can't arrest anyone they don't have evidence on. So he deleted all the evidence."

"He lied," Jake said matter-of-factly "according to that the FBI knows you are in Miami."

Sandra read the headline out loud 'Sandra Highworth in Miami thought erasing evidence erased her criminal activity'. Sandra re read the article and sighed heavily. She put the article on the counter next to her and looked at Jake "what do I do now?" She asked him.

Slickey walks in the room and senses some tension. She stops and looks at the two and says "Am I interrupting something?"

Sandra picks up the article and hands it to Slickey. As she reads it she looks nervous. "So wait, someone deleted you from the FBI database?"

"Yes" she said exasperated "Mike told me if they didn't have any evidence on me they couldn't arrest me. That they needed evidence for an arrest. I thought I was safe." Sandra walked over to the chairs at the dining room table and sat down. She got up again, as if she forgot something and walked out of the room. She returned after a few minutes with her phone. Slickey and Jake walk over and join her at the table. Sandra calls Mike.

Sandra: what the hell, Mike, did you see today's headline?

Mike: yeah, tough break

Sandra: What do you mean tough break!? You told me with the evidence gone I couldn't get arrested. The article says that is a load of crap.

Mike: They need probable cause to arrest you. I deleted the probable cause, unless they had paper backups.

Sandra: you ensured me that I could do what I wanted without being arrested for past things.

Mike: You hire me to help you back into the city. The police cannot erase anyone without evidence. I erased the digital evidence on you. If the FBI has paper evidence, that's not my fault. I did what they paid me to do.

Sandra hung up the phone frustrated and slammed it on the table. "I've been playing with fire," she said. "Walking around spending money, getting caught on every camera. I have my natural hair color, No disguise at all."

"Sandra," Jake interrupted her "if the FBI had anything on you, you would be arrested my now."

"Okay, so devil's advocate. Not if they know you plan to hit the auction." Slickey said.

"I told daddy my entire plan. He would make sure no one let's in the way."

"You mean the same daddy who could have kept me from getting arrested and didn't. Smiley said.

Sandra picked up her phone looking through her messages. "Daddy said he didn't know that Johnson & Jones set up a trap" Sandra showed Slickey the string of text messages between her and her father.

"Mike just texted you saying turn on the news" Slickey said. All three of them went into the family room and turned on the news. Oliver Monroe was giving a press conference on behalf of the FBI, considering the article. He explained the FBI knew Sandra was in Miami the moment she arrived and put together a task force to capture her. Because of deception with the task force's leadership, Sandra was not arrested. The Task Force is now putting together evidence to make an interesting case against Sandra. Reporters shouted out questions ' Is it true Highworth someone to delete her information in the FBI system? Is it true that you have agent scanning all of your paper evidence back into the system to compile a case? Is it true that the FBI has been watching her walk around Miami because they were told that she couldn't be arrested unless she committed another crime? Is a true the Highworth has a source within the FBI who supposed to be helping her stay one step above law enforcement? Is it true that Highworth is going to the auction of Daniel Price to steal her money?"

The questions came at Monroe fast, one after the other. Monroe told Reporters that he didn't know where they're getting their information from, but he can assure that his agents are doing the best they can to make sure that this criminal is caught and brought to Justice.

Sandra slumped down into a chair next to her "this is over," she said "there is no way Danielle will let us into her auction now. My face is everywhere, I have to stay low until I can make it out of the country."

"No" Slickey said "we are doing this. If the FBI would arrest you, they would have done it already."

Jake cut in, "it seems like they were under some false information that they know is not true."

"So what" Slickey said "this story has been running all day. If they would arrest you they would have by now. I bet they are waiting for you to hit Danielle's and arrest you then. So we stick to my plan and we will be long gone before they can get any of us."

Jake crossed the room and sat in a chair across from Sandra "wait wait wait, what plan?"

Sandra spoke up "Slickey can still get into the system. I would get a flash drive into the tech supervisor's computer so she can download her program. Once downloaded she can change Danielle's account information to mine but still have it look like nothing has changed. This would have worked except now they plaster my face over the news as an international wanted con woman and there is no way Danielle will still let me go."

Slickey walked over to Sandra and squatted down to get to her eye level "go talk to the old woman. Make up some story."

Sandra sighed, "I can't lie, she knows when I am lying. We just need to stop now and go our separate ways"

Slickey put a hand on Sandra's knee, "I don't have anyone or anything to go to. This is all I got. Go talk to the lady and tell her some story that has a bit of truth in it. I don't know Sandra, this is your expertise, not mine."

"Ease up Slickey" Jake said "even if we can convince Danielle to still let us go to the auction Sandra cannot get your program into the building."

"Slickey stood and stood angled towards Sandra and Jake "yeah but you can" she said. "

'And how do you suppose I do that?" he asked snarky.

Slickey threw her hands up exasperated, "I don't know. I hack, you two are the cons. We are doing this, you two owe me that. So get your shit together and come up with a plan," she said right before storming off.

Jake stood up, crossed the room and sat by Sandra "we don't owe her anything" he whispered.

"No, Jake," Sandra said, "I owe her. I was sure that daddy knew I was back in the city and he would protect me. But the news makes it seem like the FBI knew I was here the whole time, not just daddy. And then it's like Slickey walked right into a trap. The police were there two seconds after she got locked out of her computer. All this makes little sense."

"Do you want to continue or not" Jake asked her.

"I feel like I have to" Sandra whispered.

Jake sat back in the chair and crossed one leg over the other "okay then, let's talk it out. How do we make it happen?"

"First, I need to see where Danielle's head is at" Sandra said.

"She knows our actual names, so it's safe to assume that she will believe the stories."

"I have to approach her, but if I walk up to her and start asking questions she will definitely believe all the stories." Sandra checked the wall clock. "She is sitting outside around this time." Sandra stood up and looked around.

"Wait, what's happening?" Jake asked.

"I am doing what I well" Sandra replied and walked out the room.

Danielle Price sat on her front patio in her armchair. She had jazz playing in the background through her phone. She looked over and saw Sandra walk out of her house and lay a blanket on the front lawn. This will interest, she thought. "Sandra dear" she yelled and waved her hand in a beckoning motion.

Sandra looked up and waved "Hello Danielle" she said in her French accent. Sandra walked over into the other woman's yard. "Lay it on me," Sandra said "I know you've heard the news."

"You're closer now," Danielle said "enough with the accent, have a seat"

Sandra sat down "everything they have said about me isn't true."

"Tell me what parts are true. I already know you lied about your name. What else are you lying about?" Danielle said.

Sandra looked around and sat in a folding chair that was a near Danielle "I did uh steal things-"

A chuckle cut her off "steal. That's minimization, isn't it?"

"I have not been convicted of my past crimes. I took a risk in coming back to Miami but wanted to be close to home, to my family. The life I lead is lonely, and it helps when I have facades around me."

"You changed your name so you could live in plain sight, huh? So what are you going to do now?" Danielle asked, looking off in the distance.

"I am not sure. One part of me is like to live this bubble I built until they pop it. Then there is another part of me saying self-preservation and run." Sandra was looking at Danielle trying to read the woman but got nothing.

"Well, you need to get caught and pay for your crimes. That's real simple and fair. With that being said, there is no harm in living in your so-called bubble until that happens." Danielle said, still not making eye contact.

Sandra looked at her stunned "you want me to wait around

until I get arrested?" she asked her voice going up one or two octaves.

"You have two options, my dear. I am saying the first option is the best option." Danielle peered at Sandra out of the corner of her eye "you have committed a crime, you need to pay for that."

"Danielle you don't understand, I have stolen a lot of things. This won't be just a slap on the wrist, I will go to prison"

Danielle turned, so that she was looking back out across her neighborhood "you should've thought about that before you stole people's livelihood dear."

Sandra sat back in the chair, defeated. "I understand if you don't want me to come to your auction anymore" she said a whisper.

"Oh no, I called the company in charge of my auction and they assured me they have already stopped an attempt for from someone trying to gain access to my account and I have nothing to worry about. You should come still, live your bubble to the fullest."

"I can't believe you still trust me to attend" Sandra said looking at Danielle.

"Like I said dear, my money is not in jeopardy. Even if you would steal it, you won't now that I know who you are, right?" Danielle said looking straight at her.

"Yes, ma'am" Sandra said and sat back in her chair.

Danielle stared at Sandra for a few more moments and then sat straight in her chair. "Go on ahead about your business now" she said as she gathered her belongings and headed towards her house.

Sandra sat there stunned, "they have dismissed me." Sandra got up and walked over to her yard. She thought over the conversation she just had and the abrupt departure. Danielle sits outside every day around the same time but this felt like she was waiting to talk to Sandra and once she got what she wanted, she was done. Sandra wrapped her blanket up and headed in the house.

Jake was standing in the living room waiting for her "what did she say?"

Sandra came in and threw the blanket on the closest hard surface "they do not kick us out, she said that since she knows I am thief now, I wouldn't dare steal anything from her."

Jake lit up "that's good, right? Now we can move on to the next part."

"Yeah, I guess" Sandra shook her head "okay so I cannot contact the tech guy"

Jake started walking over to the couch and sat down. He pulled over his laptop and pulled up his screen he had been working on. He motioned to Sandra to come over. She walked over and sat next to him, looking at his screen.

"This is the guy" he said pointed to the screen. "I did some research, with the help of Slickey we discovered he is a 55-year-old who had worked with this company for all the eight years they have been open. He works from a laptop and desktop computer. We are not sure if he carries the laptop around with or not. If he does, this will be easy. If he doesn't we will need some rouse to get into his office at work."

"So how are we going to get to him?" Sandra asked. After a moment of thinking, she answered her own question: "we need a reason to show up at his house." She stood up and paced a three foot space in front of her. "Where does he live?" she asked.

Jake picked up his phone and texted Slickey. In a few minutes she came down the stairs and sat next to him. He passed over his computer, and she began typing.

"He lives in Miami" she said and told the address. "It's an apartment building." Slickey pulled up google maps and input the address. "It has no doorman or anything like that."

"What services does he have coming to his house? Or does he have a complaint open to his property manager," Sandra asked.

Slippery went clicking away on her computer. After a few minutes of silence she said, "he is waiting for a plumber for his sink."

Both Slickey and Sandra looked at Jake "can you fix a sink" Sandra asked.

"There is nothing YouTube and Google can't fix."

"Okay," Sandra said "let's wait for Saturday, because if he takes his laptop home it will be there on the weekend."

"I'll change the ticket to complete so the property manager doesn't send someone else before we get there." Slickey said and continued to type on the computer. Slickey looked over at Jake "I'll have the program ready by tomorrow, I'll give it to you on a flash drive. All I need you to do is put it in the computer, wait 30 seconds and then take it out and flush it."

"Got it" Jake said.

Danielle went back into her house and went up to her room. She picked up her landline and then dialed a number. The phone rang three times before someone picked up "detective Michaels" the man on the other line said.

Danielle told the detective about her conversation with Sandra once they finished her the detective said "Thank you for your cooperation ma'am. If you could, please keep the relationship open with Ms. Highworth and let her go to your auction. We are working hard to arrest her there."

"No problem, young man," Danielle said.

"We also appreciate you keeping our conversations confidential." Michaels said.

"No problem young man" Danielle said "I understand." She hung up the phone.

Follow the trail

Rodriguez and Firestone was on their way to the bureau building. Firestone looked over at Rodriguez "how are you holding up?" he asked.

"She is not dead, there is no way for me to be holding up. We will find her." she said very snappy, keeping her attention on the road.

"Yes, we will find her. You still can be hurt or sad."

"I don't have time for upset or sad" Rodriguez said as she parked and opened the car door.

They both exited the car and walked into the building. Firestone followed Rodriguez so that he wouldn't have to do the visitors line. They headed upstairs to the conference room. They were the first ones to arrive. Rodriguez sat and pulled her notes out and prepared to present her findings. She sat there with her legs bouncing up and down eager to get the meeting over with.

"What's wrong, chill out Rodriguez," Firestone said.

"We shouldn't be here. We should follow leads."

"What leads do we have?" he asked her. "I am not trying to upset you but we need help on our next move will be."

Rodriguez huffed and sat back in her chair. The rest of the

team filed in and everyone sat around waiting for Monroe and Dominguez to come into the room. Everyone sat there having small conversations. Monroe walked into the room first and greeted everyone. "Who posted bail?" he asked getting right down to business.

Clearweather spoke up "according to what we found, the FBI did."

"The FBI did what?" Dominguez said when he walked in.

"The account that the money to bail Macwire out came from an FBI account." Clearweather said more. "So I went to accounting and talked to Barb. She told me that the account that was used was a general account everyone from one from Supervisory Special agents and up have access to. She couldn't tell me who it was. All she could say is that the reason listed for the charge is releasing a crucial witness." Belle said.

Dominguez put his finger up in a 'just a moment' gesture and pulled out his phone. He spoke to his secretary giving her directions to get the name of the individual who used the account and put in the reasoning. "we train them not to give out the specific information" he said speaking to the group. "It stops people getting information it does not clear them to get. I will get things moving." he continued.

Michaels spoke up "I got a call from Danielle Price today. She told me she had a conversation with Sandra where she admitted the stories were true but said she came back to Miami to hide out and not feel lonely. She still will attend the auction I told her to keep our conversations private and we will work out when and where to arrest her. She also told me that when Highworth 1st moved into the neighborhood, she told everyone her name was Jane Stoneybrooke. She has a husband Smith Stoneybrooke. This matches the financial information we got from Rodriguez last week. Jane is a made up person however she is saying she is the heir to Miriam Stoneybrooke, who just moved to France. Miriam is an actual person, but she does not have a daughter, or any kids."

"The real estate agent gave us an update saying she is still having time getting information on the house Jane Stoneybrooke is supposed to be selling in France. The contract says she has two more weeks before she can void and get possession of the house back. She said she speaks to Highworth and is not concerned about this, that she is sure things will work out."

"In two weeks Highworth will be long gone and she will have possession of the house." Monroe stated.

Dominguez cut in "who is Smith Stoneybrooke?"

"Facial recognition has the guy who has been seen with Highworth as Jake Blaten." Belle said. "Michaels gave us his surveillance notes, and it seems like Blaten is thought to be living in the same house."

I don't know who the leak is" Monroe said 'I will find out though. There is not many people who know that there is a task force, let alone the details of the investigation. What I can tell you is Sandra Highworth is Jackson's daughter."

Rodriguez stood up "his daughter! So he is behind all of this? Telling us she couldn't be arrested, getting her hacker out of jail, Jelena getting kidnapped."

"Hold on," Dominguez said "we have no evidence that Jackson is in any way connected to the disappearance of Cohert. Have a seat so we can continue Rodriguez."

Rodriguez took her seat enraged. Her leg bounced up and down nonstop.

Monroe continued, "The task force was started to keep his eye on his daughter I believe. There is a plane ticket with

Sandra's name on it, in his personal email account. The ticket is for September 8th. Which is what I believe to be the original date of the auction? The destination is to the Bahamas, one way."

Dominguez spoke up "All we know for sure at this point is that Jackson is Sandra's father and that he started this investigation for unknown reasons. Everything else is speculation until we have evidence. Monroe will keep pursuing this angle."

Monroe walked over to an empty chair in the room and sat down. "What else do we have on Highworth?"

Jonathan "we can keep doing surveillance. We also need to know her alternative plan. Is it possible to get a bug in the house? We know Macwire cannot and will not try to hack into Jones & Johnson's system the same way she did the last time."

"How do we know she will even stick around?" Rodriguez said irritated "she's free now, she might run."

Monroe looked at Rodriguez "don't push it Agent Rodriguez." He shifted his attention to look over the group "she was bailed out, her charges were not dropped. She will still face criminal charges for her crime." He then looked at Jonathan "we need more surveillance. I will work on getting warrants for bugs. Thanks to the news she knows almost as much as we do. We know from Ms. Price that she still plans on attending the auction. We need to know her plan. I need you to follow her and Blaten, split up to cover more ground. You can either take the weekend and grind now or take this day and a half and grind the weekend, your choice. Check in is Monday morning."

Jonathan and Michaels got up and left the room. "What do you want to do?" Michaels said.

"How do we figure out what the alternative plan is?" Jonathan said.

"We have been grinding all week. Whatever they have planned you think something will happen today or tomorrow?" Michaels asked.

"We can start again Saturday morning." Jonathan said "I don't know what good surveillance will do without bugs though. You know what bugs me though," Jonathan said "that they always send us out of the room before they talk about what's going on with Cohert."

Michaels looked at him "I'll text firestone for information and let you know. Why don't you text Rodriguez?"

"She and I are not close like that, you know, we only speak at work type thing."

"Ahh, okay gotcha'" Michaels responded "We will meet up at HQ to get that other car at 7am on Saturday, sound good?"

Jonathan signed and sucked his teeth "Yeah, see you then." The two got off the elevator and headed towards the door and to their prospective cars.

Dominguez spoke up "where are we on my girl?" he said.

Firestone didn't even attempt to speak first. He sat back in his chair and let Rodriguez take it.

"We have retraced her steps" she started "she got attacked and then got the threatening text message. She traced the text message to a burner phone and ended up at a convenience store. The manager remembered her and let her search the receipts. That's where she got three names to run. According to her notes she got the three names because they bought a burner phone in the time since she was attacked and paid with a card.

She interviewed Frank Kinckade first. She notes multiple things during this interview. One being he knew she was an FBI agent before she introduced herself. She described him as charming and manipulative. He tried to flirt with her but got frustrated when she caught him up during her questioning and changed from charming to abrupt and kicked her out. When we interviewed him he said he remembered the gent coming to talk to him but doesn't remember the details. He was not flirtatious or charming during the interview. He answered the question and said no more or no less. He invited us in but did not invite us past the front hallway area. His alibi for the day she got abducted was he went running early in the morning in his neighborhood then to the grocery store. He came straight home from that and didn't leave again. He couldn't remember any times. This was one thing Jelena noted was inconsistent when she interviewed him. I asked him how he knew she was an agent before she introduced himself and he denied he did.

Mark Holmes was her next suspect. Her notes showed she believed he was having a marital affair, and that was the reason he bought the burner phone. When we went to interview him, he would not let us in the house. He said the last FBI agent who came to his house messed up his marriage. We left asking no questions.

There was a last name on the list that she did not have time to go talk to. We followed up at the address, and no one was home. We went downstairs to get any preliminary findings about the things found at the scene." Rodriguez choked on that last word. "They told us there was DNA left on her purse that was being analyzed. Since we know Kinckade bought a phone and has no real alibi is that enough to search his apartment?"

"No" Monroe and Dominguez said at the same time. Monroe let his father speak "we need something that ties Kinckade to Cohert or the attack. What makes you so certain it is him?"

"Just a feeling, sir. Also, but the looks of Jelena's notes she did not believe him either."

"Let's pull him in for questioning," Monroe said "see if he says anything that will trip him up."

Rodriguez got up and left the room. Firestone stood up and said goodbye to the others in the room and exited.

Dominguez looked at Clearweather and Belle "you two have it easy for the next few days check in on Monday unless we have a break in Jelena's case."

The rest of the gentlemen in the room got up and left after saying a few pleasantries. Mr. Kinckade had set up a time to go in for an interview the next morning and Rodriguez struggled with there being nothing she could do but wait. "Come on" Firestone told her "Let's takes the files back to your place and go back over Jelena's notes. Maybe we missed something that would help."

Rodriguez looked at him relieved he would not tell her to relax or something. She smiled at him and exhaled "thanks" she said. They gathered the materials from Rodriguez cubicle and headed out.

Kinckade has been calling Jackson all day. Why wasn't he answering? Kinkcade gave and called the other cell number he had for him. When Jackson didn't answer he called his office phone enraged. Kinkcade got the answering machine "Jackson you better call me back. Why am I being called into do questioning with the FBI? Do your fucking job and keep me out of this. I finished what you couldn't now it is your turn."

He finished leaving the message and then slammed the phone on the counter. Kinckade sat there for a few minutes and then regretted his actions. He didn't know who would listen to that message. What was he thinking? Kinckade paced the room trying to think of what to do next. Should be run or go to the interview. Running would be suspicious. Could he trust Jackson to keep him out of this? No, he could not. He would just have to get himself out of it like he always did. First, he needed to solidify his alibi.

Monroe was sitting at Jackson's desk messing around with his computer as the phone rang. He decided not to answer it but let it ring and would listen to the voicemail message. Once the blue light started beeping he pressed a button and listened to the message. He looked at the caller ID and ran the number that called he smiled when the name came up Frank Kinckade. Monroe picked up the phone and dialed his dad's personal number. When he picked up, he told him about the phone call and voicemail. "Save it and send it to yourself" Dominguez said "we can get a warrant for a search for devices used to contact Jackson under our suspicion that he is helping Highworth. If we find anything there that ties to Jelena it will be a bonus. Do we know if Jackson knows about this voicemail?"

"No, sir" Monroe said.

"Find out" Dominguez said and then hung up the phone.

Monroe sent text messages to the task force informing them they had enough for the search warrant and the address.

35 minutes later the task force and FBI crime scene investigators showed up at Frank Kinkade's house. He was not home so had to call the property manager to come open his door. Rodriguez had her gloves on and got to work.

"We need someone to find out when trash day is and go through his trash can and the dumpster," Monroe said.

The team searched for 3 hours before one tech called Monroe "There is something you should see sir." Monroe and the task force went to the kitchen to look where the tech was referring to. In a drawer here were at least 10 burner phones.

Rodriguez directed her statement at Firestone "pick them up and start calling my number. I know the number of the phone used to call Jelena."

Firestone did as told, while the others picked up a phone to search its history. Jonathan had a phone in his hand and went to settings to find the phone number the phone used. As he stared at it Rodriguez was barking at him to hand it over. Jonathan read of the number to Rodriguez and asked her did the number sound familiar.

"No, that's not the number that called her," Rodriguez said.

Jonathan then went to call history and looked through it. "There are a lot of calls from two specific numbers" Jonathan and read off the first number.

"Wait" Monroe said "that sounds similar to my work number." He searched through his phone and found Jackson's work cell phone number and read it off, it matched.

"So what is the other number," Rodriguez asked.

"Don't know" Monroe said "call it and find out."

When they called the number no one answered, but a voicemail kicked it. 'This is Jackson, leave a message' and then he ended the call.

"Wait" Rodriguez spoke up confused "both numbers belong to SSA Jackson?"

"He has a personal number and a work number." Monroe said. He dialed his father's number "Hola papí" he said once Dominguez answered. "We are here and we have multiple burner phones. We haven't tied one to Jelena yet but we have one that has called Jackson's work cell phone and personal cell phone."

Dominguez was silent for a few moments. "So we have an

angry voicemail that connects Kinckade to Jackson. We have cell phone logs that connect Kinckade to Jackson. Have one of your guys push the paperwork to get Jackson's phone logs, every phone he owns. Send it to me and I will push it through."

Monroe hung up the phone and looked at Belle and Clearweather. "Hey, go back to the bureau building and get a request for all of Jackson's call logs. We need the wording to include every phone he owns."

Belle and Clearweather nodded and headed off. A tech came into the apartment dirty and smelling like trash "uh, sir," he said. Everyone turned around and looked at the tech. "We found this in the trash sir." He held up an evidence bag with a broken cell phone in it. Rodriguez rushed forward and grabbed the evidence bag. "How do we get the number off she asked the tech who was taken aback by the force in which Rodriguez took the evidence bag out of his hand"?

"Uhh, there is a model number on the back of the phone. We could either call the warehouse or ask them to look it up, or wait until we get back to the lab and see what we can get off of it."

Reading her mind Firestone pulled out his phone and search through for the warehouse's number. Rodriguez walked over to a table and flattened out the bag to read the model number. Firestone had the phone to his ear and was speaking to someone. He said "thank you sir, and the number is" which gave Rodriguez her cue to read the model number. After a few seconds Firestone read off a phone number. Rodriguez didn't have to check anything or write anything down, she knew it.

"There is the connection" she shouted "he did it, that's the number that texted Jelena."

The rest of the night went in a blur. A bolo went out for Frank

Kinckade. Rodriguez went back to the bureau building waiting for Frank Kinckade to be brought in. She paced she looked over notes and evidence. She bothered the tech guys for fresh information. She wrote interview questions. She went into the break room and took a nap. When she woke up Firestone was handing her a cup of coffee. She sat up and smiled "thank you." She grabbed the cup and sat up on the couch. She sipped the coffee, and they sat there in a comfortable silence.

"A few minutes later her cell phone rang. She gave it to Firestone and felt around her pockets for her phone. "Hello" she said once she got the phone to her ear."

"Yes sir – yes sir – okay on the way." She said and hung up the phone. She stood up and walked out of the room without a word. Firestone knew better than to ask questions and just followed her. They ended up at the interrogation room, and Firestone went into the adjourning room.

Kinckade sat in the steel chair looking irritated. His leg bounced up and down. His eyebrows were furrowed with his arms crossed across his chest. His eyes were shifting back and forth across the room from the two-way mirror to the door and back again. Rodriguez entered the interrogation room.

"Hello again Mr. Kinckade, I am Agent Rodriguez we spoke already"

"Yea, yea, yea" He said almost a whisper "What am I here for?"

"I'm sorry, speak up sir," She said to him in a warm voice tone "we just have to make sure the recording devices can hear you."

"Why am I here" he shouted.

Rodriguez kept her voice warm and welcoming "we just have some follow-up questions for you and we have recent information we would like to clear up with you."

Kinckade glared at her "you act like I have a choice" spitting the last few words.

"Just checking your alibi for this past Saturday, can you repeat it for me, please?"

Kinckade signed and jerked back in his chair. Keeping his arms crossed and his right leg bouncing. "I woke up, went for a run and then grocery shopping. I do not know the time frames. I was not paying attention."

"What about Wednesday, what did you do Wednesday?"

"When on Wednesday," he spat.

"Just give me an overview of the entire day," she said to him.

His eyes darted around the room, and we hesitated answering the question. "Mr. Kinckade" she said. "Do you need me to repeat the question?"

"I don't remember what I did yesterday." he snapped

"Are you sure? It would help us out."

"Why would I want to help you out" he slammed his hands on the table.

Rodriguez smiled "as you stated sir, you don't have a choice. So if you would please."

"I do not remember what I did, you guys took my phone so I cannot look at my calendar. The honest answer is I do not know." he said sneering at her.

"How many burner phones do you have Mr. Kinckade?" Rodriguez said smiling from her eyes.

"I do not have any burner phones." he said not looking at her.

"Ya know the track phones, minute phones. You don't own any of those?"

Kinckade went to reply and they hesitated "Uh, I buy a few

of them. I do not know how many I have."

"Why do you have over one?" Rodriguez asked.

"I use them for my job."

"Which job is that?"

"I do construction work. When I get day laborer I dislike giving them my number, so I buy burners. Is there something wrong with that?" he sneered at her.

She ignored his question and asked him, "How do you know SSA Jackson?"

Kinckade looked at her and smiled "why are we talking about other men. Let's keep this between me and you."

Rodriguez leaned forward over the table "you're evading my question Kinckade."

Kinckade leaned forward over the table to match Rodriguez" posture "Jackson Is an old friend. I haven't spoken to him a while though."

"You sure, According to you're 'work' phones," she put in quotation marks "you have spoken to him veryntly."

Kinckade sat back in his chair and crossed his arms "Oh yea, I forgot about that."

"What was the conversation about?"

"I am not sure I remember" Kinckade said.

"You called him often. From two different phones. It had to be something important right?"

Kinckade sneered at her "well it seems like you know the answers to all your questions. So why am I here?"

Rodriguez smiled at him "I just need to hear things in your own words."

"How are these for my own words, I want a lawyer" he drawled, enunciating each word. Kinckade smiled at her.

Rodriguez stood and walked around the table and stood next

to Kinckade "Mr. Kinckade stand up please" she said.

He looked at her with surprise "for what?"

Rodriguez placed her hand around his biceps, helping him stand up. She placed his hands around his back "Frank Kinkcade you are under arrest for the attack and kidnapping of Jelena Cohert. You may remain silent, anything you say can and will be used against you in a court of law. You have the right to an attorney, if you cannot afford one, one will be provided for you. Do you understand these rights as I have said them?"

"Wait, you cannot arrest me, you have no evidence. Hold on, I need to speak to Jackson."

Rodriguez repeated "do you understand these rights as I have said them to you?"

"Yes" he screamed "I understand my right. I am not going anywhere without speaking to Jackson."

Rodriguez looked at the two-way mirror and Firestone took his cue and came around to the interrogation room. Firestone opened the door and looked at Kinckade.

"Hold on" Kinckade said. "Just hold on, let me speak to Jackson."

"Sir," Firestone said in a deep, intimidating voice "you have revoked your right to counsel and have been Mirandize Right now you are resisting arrest and need to follow the directions that are being given to you."

Kinkade's eyes got wide with rage. He began walking towards the door with Rodriguez following him. Firestone let them walk out first before he followed. They met some unis in the hallway and gave Kinckade to them to be transported to booking. Rodriguez turned to Firestone "we still need to find Jelena."

They walked towards Rodriguez' cubicle "well we know he didn't have her at his apartment. He must have another property somewhere where he is holding her." Firestone said.

Once they got there Rodriguez picked up the phone and called Gretchen "Hey Gretchen" she was when the other women picked up her phone.

"Hey Hun, what can I do for you?"

"Can you do a check for me? See what properties a Frank Kinckade has listed under his name."

There was clicking on the other end of the phone. "He has an apartment, but I'm guessing you all already knew that." Gretchen continued clicking on the computer. "I bet what you didn't know if that he owned the building."

Firestone was in the background taking notes "Wait it's his building that he is living in?"

"Yes, Ma'am," Gretchen said. There was a few moments of silence "that's all dear. No other properties under his name. Anything else?"

There were a few moments of silence and then Firestone said "Hey Gretchen this is Detective Firestone MDPD. Just on a hunch can you tell us the properties that SSA Jackson owns?"

Rodriguez looked at him but she knew what he was thinking. These two are linked somehow. It would be crazy to think that Jackson was giving Kinckade space to hurt Jelena.

"Uh, sure" Gretchen said, feeling some hesitancy that Rodriguez felt. After a few clicks she said "He has an apartment in the city," she supplied the address "and he has a house out in Great Palms listed. It says here he rents it out though. And before you ask, there is a current tenant named David Chopper but the utilities are being paid for my SSA Jackson."

Firestone wrote the address Gretchen supplied. They thanked

her and then hung up the phone. "Let's take it to Monroe, if he says I'm stretching then I'll let it go. I just have the feeling he is more involved than a couple phone calls. You see how Cohert embarrassed him in front of all of us last week." he told Rodriguez.

"Yea but he knew Dominguez in Jelena's father. He is mad enough to put out a hit on her is a bit of a stretch. We can go see what Monroe thinks though."

The two of them walked to Monroe's office and knocked on the door. When they arrived both Monroe and Dominguez were there "sorry for the interruption sir, we have a theory to run past the both of you."

Dominguez gestured her and Firestone to come in. They entered the room and Rodriguez started "Kinckade lawyered up, we arrested him and sent him with the unis. We went to go talk to Gretchen, and he doesn't own any other properties besides the building he lives in."

"Wait" Monroe said "he owns the building he lives in?"

"Yea, So on a hunch Firestone got a list of properties Jackson owns. He has an apartment in the city and he owns a place he rents out in Great Palms." Rodriguez' eyes got wide as she remembered something. "I remember talking to Jelena about a woman going missing in Great Palms. It's up to like 5 of them so far. Could that be a coincidence? Do we have enough for a search warrant?"

Monroe asked "does the house in the burbs have a tenant?"

"Yes sir," she said "his name is David Cooper, but the utilities are being paid for by Jackson."

Monroe looked at Dominguez and Dominguez said "we have enough to search all his properties based on us what Monroe uncovered about his knowledge of Sandra's whereabouts. Gather your teams send one team to the apartment and you and the task force go to great Palms.

Monroe, Rodriguez and Firestone headed out. Rodriguez texted Jonathan and Belle on the way with the address for them to meet them at. Everyone arrived at the address in Great Palms and walked to Monroe when he got out of his car.

"Crime scene unit is on the way along with a few techs. They are running behind no one gave them the word that we have two locations."

"What's the plan" Rodriguez asked "Are we waiting?"

"Ya'll know how to do a search. You find anything let me know"

The group turned and went to the front door. Monroe knocked on the door, "hello, this is Oliver Monroe with the FBI open the door, please."

Everyone waited so one could tell the different octaves in the breathing. Monroe knocked one more time and repeated himself "Mr. Cooper, if you are there we have a warrant to search the premises please open the door."

The chorus of breathing happened again. Monroe waited an extra beat and then nodded. The FBI group took the cue and drew their weapons. The MDPD crew took the hint and took out their weapons. Monroe counted to three took a step back, bent his knees and kicked the door. It swung open and Rodriguez, who was first to the right of the door, entered with her weapons up and pointed. The others followed, and they spit up to search the house.

'Clear' were yelled through the house as the team went from room to room and found no one. They all made their way to the front of the house, putting their weapons away.

"She is not here" Rodriguez said with her voice cracking.

"Search the house" Monroe barked out. He pivoted to hide the glisten the tears were making in his eyes.

They put gloves on as the techs showed up and the search was underway. "I am checking the basement," Michaels said.

Stunned Monroe and Rodriguez followed his voice to his location "Did we clear this room" Monroe asked.

"I didn't even know it was here" Michaels said with Rodriguez agreeing. "I leaned against this to steady myself and it clicked and this opened."

The group drew their weapons and headed downstairs. Rodriguez understood the stairs and froze. She saw five bodies hanging upside down, tortured and beaten. She went over to the bodies just as Monroe and Michaels had cleared the area. She bent down and looked at each face searching for Jelena.

A sigh of relief when she realized they weren't Jelena, followed by the dread of all these females' lives lost. She looked around the room at all the concrete. The floor was damp, there were chains in the middle of the floor. There was a table with knives, and hooks and other torture devices on it. In the middle of the floor it was a glass of water and saltine crackers... In the middle of the floor was a bloody knife. The tears streamed down Rodriguez' face

"Let's let the techs process down here" he said putting an arm around her guiding her towards the stairs. Rodriguez had her head down as she let him guide her. She stopped "look" she said pointing down" a blood trail.

"It's a blood trail" Monroe said "Let's not get out hopes up. We won't know if it is hers until it gets analyzed."

Before he could even get the rest of his sentence out Rodriguez was following the trail. Up the stairs, through the house and out the front door. Monroe followed behind her, and watching her six because she was so focused. She stopped at a spot where the blood trail just ends. She looks around and sees tire tracks. Rodriguez yells for Firestone who comes running out. "Blood trail watch out" Monroe says.

Firestone realizes nothing is wrong and slows down stepping. As he approaches Rodriguez points down at the ground "what car is this?" she asks. Firestone bends down and studies the tracks. "They are wide which tells me an enormous car could be an enormous truck or a pick up. For me to know more I would need a clearer cast."

Rodriguez runs to her car. Monroe follows behind her, finding out that he needs to ask questions later. Rodriguez yells "get everyone else. We need a search in the immediate area. He took her in a car. She is out there somewhere."

The group drove around until 2pm Friday afternoon. They were tired, most of them had worked through Thursday night. They were discouraged because they had not found Jelena. Monroe was about to call it quits. They were in a brush area about 1 mile from the property searching through the foliage. A woman came over to them "Excuse me" the elderly lady said. Both Rodriguez and Monroe looked up. Rodriguez ignored her and continued to look.

The lady looked at Monroe said "you are police right?"

"Yes ma'am" Monroe said happy for the distraction.

"I've found a young lady over here a few days ago. I don't have a car so I couldn't get her to a hospital. I used to be a nurse so I am trying to take care of her but I was just going to call 911. I believe I bit off more than I could chew this time."

Both Monroe and Rodriguez raced towards the women "show us your house" they said in unison. The lady looked surprised and then turned and led them to her house. On the way Monroe called for medics to meet them at the address. When they arrived, the lady opened the door and there was Jelena laying on a cot with a cloth wrapped around her breast and her underwear on. They hooked her up to an IV and had stitches everywhere. "I am sorry I don't have all the proper equipment" the lady said.

Monroe and Rodriguez started crying. Monroe rushed to his sister and checked her pulse on her neck. "Barley a pulse" he said out loud. Rodriguez was stuck in place crying. She couldn't make her self-move towards Jelena, she couldn't make herself back away. She only moved when the EMT's came in a brushed her out of the way. Within minutes Jelena was being carried away, and tech guys were processing the woman's house. The entire team arrived and Monroe gave orders

"I will call my father and Firestone, Rodriguez and I will go to the hospital. I need Michaels and Jonathan on Highworth. When word gets out she is in the hospital, if Highworth is behind it she could make a move. We got the warrant for bugs, get them into her house. Maybe use Danielle Price."

The two men left the scene and went to their cars. "We could take shifts," Jonathan said. We didn't get any time to sleep or do anything before we got a text message."

"Naw, I'm fine" Michaels looked at Jonathan "are you?"

They both stopped at the car with hands on the handles "Let's go" Michaels said.

Monroe looked at Clearweather and Belle "I will send you my files,, on Jackson. I need tight cases tying Kinckade to Jelena and Kinckade to Jackson. If Jackson is behind what Kinckade did to my sister, find it."

"When do we check in?" Clearweather asked.

"Monday" Monroe said and then walked to his car, He yelled to the officers "I need the old lady questioned. Something is not right." and then pulled off.

The team split up and went their separate ways.

She's alive, but will she live?

In the hospital Jelena went directly into surgery. Dominguez, Monroe, Rodriguez and Firestone waiting in the allotted waiting room for hours. Coffee was fetched, sandwiches were delivered. Phones were played on, died and charged. Finally, about five hours later, at 8 pm the doctor came out.

Everyone stood up and rushed over to him. "Who all do we have here?" the doctor asked.

"Just get on with it doctor" Dominguez barked.

"Okay," the doctor said calmly "Jelena just came out of surgery and is in critical condition. She was stabbed multiple times. The wounds were in different stages of healing letting me know she was tortured over a period of time. The care that was given to her prolonged her death, but she would have died if she would not have been brought in when she did. The surgery went well but I caution against this many people going in to see her right now."

Before the doctor could even get his caution out the four officers of the law were rushing towards the direction, the doctor gestured towards. Dominguez entered the room first and saw his daughter. She had bruises all over her face. Tubes came out of her nose and throat. She had bandages and different types of dressings.

Dominguez stepped forward slowly, eyes glistening with tears as he looked at his daughter's broken body. Once he approached her, he reached out as if to touch her and then pulled back. He didn't want to break her. Her eyes opened slowly "Mija" Dominguez said.

Jelena looked up at him. Her eyes searched the room "Ang" she started to say but her voice was so horse she couldn't get the other two syllables out.

"Angela rushed forward "Estoy aquí chica, I'm here." She placed her hand on her shoulder lightly and wiped the tears from falling.

"Highworth" Jelena struggled to get out before the whites of her eyes showed and the machines she was hooked up to began blinking and beeping. Doctors and nurses swarmed in and kicked everyone out.

Around nine o'clock Dominguez ordered Rodriguez and Firestone home. As they walked towards the parking lot Firestone grabbed her hand. Her hand went ridget for a moment and then she relaxed into him. They make it to the car and Cassidy asks "where to?" as they put their seatbelts on.

"I just want to sleep." Angela says. She leaned her head back on her chair and closed her eyes. Cassidy starts the engine and heads off "Home we go" she says quietly.

Monday morning the team received messages to meet in the hospital. "Take me to my car so I can get my go bag," Angela says to Cassidy.

"All the way to your car, where is it HQ or the bureau building?" Cassidy asked as he rolled back over in the bed and pulled the covers up over his head.

Angela pushed his shoulder "the only clothes I have are the ones I wore two days ago. Ya' know, when you kidnapped me and brought me here."

Cassidy pulled the cover down and peered at her over his shoulder "kidnapped you, a little dramatic, huh?"

Angela pulled back the covers and slipped on a pair of sweatpants and a hoodie she has been wearing the last few days. "Come on, we have to be at the hospital in an hour." She picked up a pillow off the bed and threw it at him. Cassidy groaned and pulled the cover back. He padded into the bathroom. Angela took the opportunity to get a cup of coffee. She turned on the Keurig and had her cup ready by the time Cassidy came out.

"What no coffee for me?" he said wearing an outfit similar to hers.

"We don't have time, let's go" she said as she headed to the door." She turned on him "wait" she held her hand up "you are wearing sweatpants and a hoodie to a debriefing, with Dominguez, the Deputy Director, have you forgotten?"

Cassidy rolled his eyes and turned and went back into his room. He emerged a few minutes later with blue jeans and brown loafers. He was wearing a light blue button-down shirt. "Better" he asked with his hands open wide?"

"You're wasting time" she said "let's go."

They left the apartment and went to his car "Where is your car?"

"It is at HQ," she replied.

At the hospital the team all gathered in Cohert's room. She was sitting up in bed, all the tubes removed. Everyone let Rodriguez enter first. She smiled widely and walked over to Cohert "te ves bien, you look good" Rodriguez said. She stopped at the side of her bed.

"Aw please Ang, I look like hell" Jelena replied. "Hey guys, come on in."

The room filled with the task force and Cohert told everyone how she was and that her recovery would be slow but she should be discharged in a couple days. "Let's get down to business," she said.

"The man who attacked me was Frank Kinckade. He kept saying that someone wanted me dead. He had five other girls," Cohert broke off.

"We see them," Rodriguez jumped in.

Cohert nodded "what do we got?"

Clearweather spoke up "Jackson called the hit on you. He knew Kinckade, he let Kinckade use the house for murdering girls. Jackson looked the other way because Kinckade was on his beck and call, doing his dirty work."

"What evidence do we have?" Dominguez asked.

"All circumstantial" Belle said "we have phone records that tie Jackson to Kinckade based on Jackson's phone records. Kinckade changes phones excessively but Jackson does not. Jackson has owned that house for 20 years. He has had a tenant named David Cooper for the past ten years. David Cooper is Kinkade's dead brother's name. The actual David Cooper had his throat cut in a cold, unsolved case."

Clearweather took over "David Cooper was the main suspect in the killing of Jackson's first wife. There was not enough evidence for an arrest, let alone a conviction. So our working theory is Cooper and Jackson had some sort of arrangement with that house that Jackson's first wife didn't like. Cooper kills the first wife to get her out of the picture. Jackson tries to do things the proper way and when they can't get enough evidence he goes to his brother to kill him, which he does and that ties Jackson and Kinckade together. There have been numerous associates of Jackson's that have gone missing over the years and not found. There are bodies being pulled up all around that house. We don't know anything for sure until the techs are done"

"So what was the trigger?" Monroe asked "that comment Cohert made to Jackson?"

"That's what we think," Belle said.

"Along with the whole Romanary thing," Cohert said.

"Me firing Romanary had part in this?" Dominguez asked?

"Fired" Rodriguez said surprise

"It was proof to him that I could make real the threat I made, even though it wasn't him. But what's going on with Highworth?"

"Jonathan and I followed Blaten from the house to the house of the head tech for Johnson and Jones. So it seems like they still are going on with the plan."

"Why did he go into his house?" Monroe asked.

"We are pretty sure he planted a bug or something. There is just no way to be sure."

"We will ask him to bring in his computer so it can be swept." Dominguez said, pulling out his phone.

"Are we sure that is what we want to do?" Monroe asked.

"What do you mean?" Dominguez

"We want to catch her right? We already took her hacker. So why would we take away yet another avenue?"

"We have no way of knowing what their new plan is, how are they planning to take the money." Dominguez countered.

"We know what they are doing and when. We have an in

with Danielle." Cohert said, "We have to keep Jackson out of it because he could warn her. The auction is on Saturday, let's get our shit together and get her."

Dominguez thought this there for a few moments "papí" Cohert said "this is the way to get her. Our cases are air tight. Once we get her stealing the money, we can arrest her."

"What if the money transfers into one of her offshore accounts before we can find a way to intercept it, how are we even going to intercept it without knowing her new plan?" Michaels jumped in.

"You all have five days to figure it out" Dominguez barked. "Rodriguez and Firestone will stay on Kinckade and Jackson. The four of you" he said looking at Clearweather, Jonathan, Michaels and Belle "figure this out, get us one step ahead." Dominguez stared at Cohert "We will bring the briefings to you, you stay and heal." He looked around the room "Keep her out of it besides the briefings."

Yes sirs echoed around the room, and everyone split up. "Gracias papá y hermano" Cohert said.

"We still care, regardless of what you think." Monroe said. Cohert averted her eyes and blinked away tears.

About the Author

Hey hey, y'all! What's up?

I'm Ashley Johnson—but if you're a fan of young adult fantasy, you might know me as Sheyanne Warren. I write mystery, suspense, and stories that keep you on the edge of your seat. Originally from Syracuse, New York, I now call Charlotte, North Carolina, home.

I have a master's degree in forensic psychology (yes, I'm fascinated by the human mind!) and spend my days shaping young minds as a middle school teacher. But long before I stepped into a classroom, I was a book-loving kid who found magic in words. When I was three, my grandparents took the TV out of my room and replaced it with a bookshelf—best decision ever! From that moment on, stories became my escape, my passion, and ultimately, my calling.

Writing has always been second nature to me, but for the longest time, I didn't realize becoming an author was *actually* within reach. It felt like an unspoken dream—something I carried in my heart without fully acknowledging. But now? I'm here, doing the thing I love, and I write with purpose.

Representation matters. It's not just a phrase; it's a commitment. I want my readers—no matter who they are or where they come from—to see themselves in the pages of my books. Whether it's a fantasy world filled with adventure or a gripping mystery with unexpected twists, I write stories that reflect the diversity and richness of real life. Because everyone deserves to be the hero of their own story.

So, if you love books that blend heart-pounding suspense, intriguing mysteries, and unforgettable characters, you're in the right place. Let's embark on this literary journey together!

You can connect with me on:
- https://www.foreversevenpress.com
- https://www.instagram.com/a.johnson.author

Subscribe to my newsletter:
- https://www.foreversevenpress.com/links

Also by Ashley Johnson

www.ingramcontent.com/pod-product-compliance
Lightning Source LLC
Chambersburg PA
CBHW020538030426
42337CB00013B/902